The Gender Paradox.

The
Gender Paradox

What it means to be a transvestite.

Jed Bland

The Gender Paradox
by J.Bland

Third Edition
Copyright 1993

Printed and published in Great Britain by
The Derby TV/TS Group
Belper, Derby

British Library Cataloguing-in-Publication Data.

Bland, Jed

Gender Paradox: What it Means to be a
Transvestite. - 3Rev.ed.
I. Title
306.77

ISBN 0 9517885 2 3

CONTENTS

THE GENDER PARADOX
DEDICATION

This book is naturally based largely on my personal experiences over half a century of life, but I would like to thank all those who offered the hand of friendship, and allowed me to plagiarise their work in my early books.

The first edition of The Gender Paradox, was derived from a talk that I gave at Derby City Hospital, thanks to the good offices of Derby CVS and the Derby Self Help Project, to whom I was introduced by Derby FRIEND.

I would like to dedicate this to all the friends that I have made, that have supported me in what I am trying to do. Many of them appear in these pages, unnamed, but I thank them for sharing a little of their lives with me and hope that they don't mind me sharing it with those who may gain a little help by reading these pages.

I'd also like to thank all those who have been kind enough to read through my original drafts and criticise constructively.

Especially, I'd like to thank a transvestite and his wife, one of the most loving couples I know, who have it to spare for those who call for help, including myself, when I needed it, using the true meaning of the word, that is, caring and sharing.

Most of all I dedicate this book to my former wife, who left me with love, and, in so doing, gave me the space to grow.

Chapter 1
INTRODUCTION

I am a transvestite. I say that not to shock anyone; it is a simple fact of my life. There is so much distorted fact, fantasy and misinformation, some by transexuals justifying their position, some by sex shops seeking to boost their trade, some by news-papers looking for a "good story", that I feel that it is time to try and set the record straight.

I suppose I am not saying anything new, but I find other books on the subject very heavy going. Somehow they seem to write in the language of their speciality and I have to thank all the people in various groups who have patiently listened to me and helped me to think in plain English. Psychiatrists and others have written all sorts of things about transvestites, over the years, but they necessarily take for their material the people that consult them, people who may well have reached the limits of desperation. The secrecy surrounding transvestism is such that it probably would not occur to such writers that there are thousands of other TV's leading happy lives, as well balanced as anybody else.

More recently there have been studies by others outside the TV community, such as "Fantastic Women", by Annie Woodhouse, but even these can only deal with those that are outgoing enough to talk about themselves. That particular book is unique, in that it is written by a feminist. She sees it as a preoccupation with the female stereotype, which, on the surface it may be, but that is only part of the story, and like many textbooks, seems judgmental.

Autobiographies by "changed over" people abound, often sensationalised in the national press. In other books, like "Geraldine, For the Love of a Transvestite", by Monica Jay, and

"A Man's Tale" by John Pepper, the transvestite must appear somewhat eccentric.

It seems that transvestism is something that affects men far more than women. The reason isn't clear but, for simplicity, throughout this book I shall, generally, refer to "he" and "him", or it will get impossibly complicated.

In its literal interpretation, the word transvestite means someone who dresses in the clothes of the opposite sex - a cross dresser. The majority of male TV's appear, in their male guise as undoubtedly masculine, they are not in the least bit effeminate. When my friends and I give our talks, we go in our best suits and ties, to show that TV's are just ordinary people. We take photographs to show that we don't dress like someone out of the Rocky Horror Picture Show, at least, not usually. After one of these talks, we were told, the comments were "Didn't they look normal!" What is normal?

There are, of course, an increasing number of transexuals, who, for one reason or another, reject their male body and lifestyle and ask for the so-called "sex-change" operation. Several have written their auto-biographies, and have hit the headlines, for various reasons. They are often referred to as "pre-op" and "post-op".

When people think of transvestites, they usually picture those gay men who dress in women's clothes for a variety of reasons, sometimes to attract straight men, but more usually in a parody of women, as in the various drag acts. The kind of TV that I am writing about is called a Heterosexual Transvestite, that is, sexually attracted to women, not men. In most cases, he is just that. It isn't usually a matter of choice. The other picture that people have, is of fetishism, men who dress for sexual satis-faction, usually concentrating on a more extreme sexual stereotype. But, though it is a strongly erotic experience for many TV's, there seems to be another strange, barely comprehended component.

The name coined by John Bancroft is Dual Role Transvestite, which sums up the situation exactly; someone who lives the life of a man quite successfully, but has an undeniable urge to dress as a woman from time to time. More than that, in many cases, to "be" a woman. There are some who "dress" very rarely, others live the role full time. Some simply dress happily at home, with the simple, uncomplicated enjoyment of a different role, while others feel the need for absolute realism, and being able to "pass" in public.

There is, of course, no such thing as a typical transvestite, yet many can relate very similar life experiences. While, on one level, transvestites are simply men who like to dress up as women from time to time, for many it is a compulsion that raises questions about the fundamentals on which our Society is based. Because it is carried on in such secrecy, it breeds fear and negative reactions.

One Sunday evening, my youngest son reacted violently to the idea of inviting my friends to the house, even though they would not be "dressed". I had no idea how upset he was about things underneath, even though on the surface he was trying to be supportive. What I hadn't realised was that although he could accept it to a point with myself, he didn't want to know about anyone else.

He stormed away to his bedroom, just as Annie Nightingale played 'Arnold Lane' on Radio 1. I had to go out to meet someone and, just as I arrived at my destination, she played 'Lola'. I thought to myself, "If she plays 'Walk on the Wild Side', that will put the tin hat on it!"

These songs embody perfectly valid views of certain more visible aspects of transvestism, but only touch the surface. The vast majority of Transvestites are totally heterosexual. Few go as far as flirting with men, and fewer still go as far as a sexual encounter. The public view of transvestism and transexualism is like two tips of a vast iceberg which comprises a large proportion of our Society. The statistics suggest that approximately one person in every hundred is a transvestite, say about 250,000 men. This figure is mind-boggling if you think of a square mile of some suburb, where it works out to about 20 or 30 TV's. Few of them come out into the open; they don't tell people about it, even their parents or their wives.

Nearly everyone, in the beginning, dresses in the most absolute secrecy, hidden from everyone, even fathers, mothers, wives and families, as we say 'in the closet'. The secrecy and guilt drives many to the most extraordinary attempts to "prove themselves a man" and many have complete emotional breakdowns or even commit suicide. When it does come out into the open, it often causes indescribable distress to TV's wives. For most of the others, it builds to an obsession, always in the back of their minds, diverting their attention from both the necessities and the enjoyments of life. For some the obsession breeds fantasies, either enactment of an imagined sexual scenario, bringing it into the open in a disastrous way, or the dream that they could become a real woman.

Some years ago, "That's Life" on BBC1 featured a Yorkshire bus driver who spent all his spare time, riding his horse, patrolling the countryside around his home, in full uniform, living in the persona of Captain Hepworth of the Roundhead army of the Civil War. The feature was handled delicately and with great empathy. As they sat outside a village pub one afternoon, the interviewer made a comment about Captain Hepworth's daily life, and the latter said something very significant, "You know, you have to separate reality and fantasy."

I have tried, in this book, to explore a wide range of issues as impartially as I can, but it is a book of questions, not answers. It explores the fantasies in transvestism and hopefully, some of the realities will emerge.

Chapter 2
IN THE CLOSET

In the June 1977 issue of the British Journal of Sexual Medicine, a psychologist called Margaret Williams, wrote:

"Again and again and again I have received letters saying the same things:

"Ever since boyhood I have had a secret wish to dress in girl's clothing; I do not know why; I am not homosexual; I wish to marry or am already married; I do not wish to change sex. I have kept this secret from parents and wife, friends."

"In complete isolation these persons have gone through thought and life patterns of remarkable similarity, and are amazed and relieved to find there are so many others like them."

"Often married with children and successful in their career they are apparently normal males and their deviance is unsuspected by relatives and friends."

It doesn't help that the public image of a transvestite is of someone like Dame Edna Everage, or Tim Curry, as Frank n'Furter in the Rocky Horror Show. Worse, it is often of a fellow being caught by the Police, walking up the road in a mini-skirt, or pinching underwear off a washing line. It is this sort of image that the media latches on to, or it portrays transvestites as charming oddities, or happy-go-lucky people, at ease with the world, enacting some esoteric ritual.

For every transvestite that goes out and about, there are hundreds, as we say "in the closet". Some just like to dress quietly at home, but many others live in the deepest guilt and emotional distress. It is so completely contrary to the behaviour expected by Society. They are frightened to death that someone will find out and, even in everyday life, it is always in the back of their minds.

When not dressing they try to forget it and pretend it isn't there, but little everyday happenings trip their memory and they get an unreasoning fear that, somehow, people can "read" them, like having the mark of Cain.

No one can keep a secret so profound to themselves, year in and year out, without it ending in emotional disturbance. Maybe, in his urge to be a woman, the TV has gone out in public and got into trouble. He could find himself exposed to the ridicule of some youths. Or, perhaps someone lays a complaint and he is arrested by the police, with the embarrassment of being taken to the station, being charged, possibly being held in custody, with the humiliation of appearing before the magistrate. For a closet TV especially, the result can be shattering, leading him to retire deeper into the closet, possibly resisting the urge with drugs from the doctor, or with alcohol.

For a wife to find her husband wearing a dress, the shock and confusion must be indescribable. Suddenly the image of the husband she loves has gone, to be replaced by some bizarre creature. If he cannot understand himself, he cannot explain it to her, and the inability to communicate can explode into violence.

To the onlooker, it may seem a trivial thing, when compared to all the many other problems in our Society, yet the answer is simple and cheap. It is communication. It is the knowledge that there are others that have gone through all the same things; the knowledge that, though unusual, it is not freakish. The trouble is that communication has to be through underground channels. I am hoping that this book will be thought well enough, not to bring me personal kudos, but for counsellors and consultants to offer their clients, as a useful piece of reading matter. I would like it to be available to those who are too frightened to join a society or approach one of the specialist shops.

In 1990, the Derby Gender Line used the facilities of the Community Media Association to produce five short advertisements, shown throughout a week on Central Television. In that week there were 150 calls to the help line, and the number stayed at around forty to seventy for some weeks afterwards. About half of the callers simply asked for a local meeting place and didn't talk about any problems they may have had. Some of the others were deeply emotional and a few were very serious. From the experience of other helplines, it is reasonable to expect that there would be many who didn't call, but made a note of the number and tucked it away in their wallet.

For the caring section of Society, such as social workers, it presents a problem when it suddenly confronts them. They are, after all, human and they have been brought up in a society where men are men and women are women. Many TV's ask to speak to another TV, but I hope that helpline workers can read this and get the understanding necessary to listen with greater empathy. Together with the Police and other services, many groups become involved with the results of the emotional distress that Transvestism can cause. The organisations that provide comfort for the bereaved are quite familiar with the situation. To the psychiatrist, his patient might be suffering from depression, or a "nervous breakdown", or whatever. Would he react sympathetically to the idea that transvestism lay behind it? If the transvestite has not declared himself, only the visible symptoms can be dealt with. But the TV doesn't say what he is. Apart from anything else he has not yet admitted it to himself.

On the other hand, the TV's erratic behaviour may have been going on for some years. He may have turned to alcohol. By this time his wife may be pretty fed up with it all. But how can he explain the unexplainable? A sharp word at the wrong moment, and he reacts by striking out. To the Social Worker and the Police, he is an alcoholic and a wife-beater. Would they believe that transvestism lay behind it?

One evening, the Derby TV/TS Group received a phone call from a nurse. She didn't say which hospital she was working for, or where she obtained the Group's phone number. She said that she regularly nursed people who had attempted to commit suicide, and would talk to them and comfort them. She said "What do I say? What is it all about? Many of the men are admitted wearing items of female clothing."

If a transvestite commits suicide, he is washed and tidied up and nothing more is said, to save further distress to the family. It would appear, on reading the Gender Dysphoria Trust's booklet, "The Reality", that there is a deliberate policy for the Police and Ambulance forces and Coroners Courts not to record the incidence of cross-dressing in cases of suicide. This may be a well meaning attempt to protect the relatives, but it means that we do not have a clear idea of the numbers involved, which could be very large. The Trust suggests a figure of 1 in 5 transexuals, but their definition of a transexual is not very clear.

What about all those who don't quite reach the point of suicide? Should people really have to go to the limits of desperation before they get help and understanding? Surely there must be ways, in common humanity, that we can alleviate the situation? Even from a mercenary viewpoint, a suitable course of action could save a drain on scarce finances and resources of the NHS, Social Services and other agencies.

A few years ago, Gay Byrne's radio phone-in talk show, on Radio Telefis Eirann, turned to transvestism. After various calls giving a range of opinions and attitudes, there came a call from a woman whose transvestite husband had committed suicide only weeks before. He had hanged himself because of the sense of shame and humiliation he felt all the time. He had been a very out-going, jovial person, a good husband and father. His wife sobbed her heart out and said her biggest regret was that Transvestism had never been discussed at any great length by the media in the past. She felt that discussion would have led to a better understanding of the subject so that her husband would not have had to live in fear of anybody discovering his secret.

Chapter 3
GENDER AND SEXUAL PREFERENCE

It would be reasonable to suppose that a transvestite dresses as a woman, because he wishes to be attractive to men. But few TV's ever think along those lines when they dress, certainly not in the early days.

A helpline recently received a call from a schoolboy who had been taught in class that cross-dressing is something that gay people do. He was in enough trouble, emotionally, as it was. The thought that he might also be gay was more than he could stand. Since he was under 18, the helpline felt it could do little more than ask him if he thought he was gay, then divert him on to talk of cricket and football.

The Sunday name for such transvestism and transexualism is Gender Dysphoria. In the dictionary, dysphoria is a feeling of being ill-at-ease, an unusually apt description, although professional usage is much more limited, to those who, throughout their lives, are said to "see" themselves as being of their opposite sex. What is more difficult is the definition of Gender. It is the property of "being" a man or a woman, the lifestyle, the role, all the little ways of behaving. Some professionals suggest that one has a Gender Identity, the clear knowledge that one is a man or a woman. There is tremendous controversy over whether one is born with it or whether it develops soon after. Someone like myself is said to be confused about it, although I would say, simply, that there is a difference between what I feel I am, and what I feel I am supposed to be.

How is it that, if the transvestite is enacting the female role, why does he not take it all the way? In fact, there seems to be no reason to suppose that there are any more homosexual TV's than there are among any other group of people. For those that dress for sexual reasons, the motive is usually auto-erotic. That is, the end product is masturbation.

But, if that was the only reason, I wouldn't be writing this book. Nobody seems to be able to tell for sure is what it is in us that may cause us to be deeply distressed by the behavioural role decreed for our body shape, nor can they say, for sure, why our sexual preference may not coincide with it either. At least one in every ten people is attracted sexually to their own sex exclusively, in preference to the opposite one.

Because I see a genuine difference between being gay and being a transvestite, I would like to divert a little and describe what I see of the gay community. To my mind, being gay is not necessarily synonymous with homosexuality. There are "men who like to make love to men" as a sexual exercise rather than emotional bond. Either they refuse to acknowledge themselves as gay or they simply don't see themselves that way. Often they look for partners in "cottages", with all the attendant dangers, not to mention the fact that they are breaking the law. It should be said that some of these people simply don't feel the need to "come out" into the gay community, while others snatch secret assignations, unknown to their families. I once met a man who had been happily married for thirty years and had attempted to satisfy his need for men on occasional trips away from home.

Yet another motivation occurred to me when watching a television play where the murder victim had been involved in a homosexual encounter. It seemed to me, that it was not just a sexual thing, he was satisfying an unconscious desire for power over other men, an illustration of how all sorts of emotional needs become mixed up with sexual needs.

This is not an uncommon thing in "straight" society, of course, where feelings of "not coping" on the part of a man, may cause him to "put down" women, or indulge in practices which debase them.

There is a long tradition of cross-dressing in the theatre. In Shakespeare's day, boys acted the female roles, because it was not felt seemly for a woman to do so. In pantomime, the principal boy is a girl and the dame is a man. Throughout the history of Music Hall, there have been female impersonators. A few of my readers will remember Old Mother Riley and her daughter Kitty, played by Lucan and McShane, a husband and wife duo. In America, there was Charlie's Aunt. On television we have Danny LaRue and Dame Edna Everage. Many such artistes do not talk about themselves and do not see themselves as transvestites, but entertainers. A common feature of their act is that they satirise women or parody a particular stereotype, but then, to act as an ordinary, everyday woman would not have much point.

The most visible gay transvestites are, of course, those that set out to be "camp" in their manner, and the "drag queens" that appear in night clubs as entertainers. Almost always, at some point in their act, they make sure you know they are a man. They may, for instance, take off their wig during their act. "The Rocky Horror Show" has a cult following, with the lead role, Frank n'Furter, camping it up gloriously, but it is guaranteed to make many closet TV's cringe with embarrassment. Transvestites do not dress for laughs, they do it as an, often unconscious, need to find fulfilment in the expression of emotions and feelings that they otherwise keep buried inside them.

Few people outside the gay community know much about gay people. Most of what they are told is the myths that are promoted by the media. Little boys are continually warned to be on their guard about men in toilets. I think that, perhaps, many "straight" men are afraid of gay people. The idea of entering a gay pub or club would appal them, perhaps they would feel that they were likely to be propositioned as soon as they stepped through the door and wouldn't know how to cope with it. It is important to disabuse the TV of this idea, if he is about to 'come out', because many meetings are held in gay venues, if they are such that, as another minority group, we are accepted. I remember at one regular meeting, we had the distinct feeling that the gay clientele were more worried by us than we were by them, possibly because they didn't know how to deal with us. It should be pointed out that not all gay venues will accept TV's, and some gay people are even more averse to TV's and TS's than straight people are. This is especially true of the more aggressive lesbians, because we stand for the very things they reject. At a nightclub in Sheffield, I remember seeing three lesbians looking in bemused puzzlement at the TV's and tut-tutting to themselves. In general, however, we are accepted. In any case, some venues are regularly patronised by "straight" people, because they feel that there is less chance of a fight breaking out. Another point to make, is that most gay helplines, such as FRIEND, know of transvestites they can call on, so if there is not a local TV line, someone can call the gay one.

The idea that all gay people indulge in random promiscuous sex is another myth. Many gay relationships are of long term, and the couple genuinely fall in love with each other. As Oscar Wilde put it: "The love that dare not speak its name." As in any other part of Society, relationships can be long term, open, promiscuous or solitary. The fact that relationships tend to be short term may be due to the pressures of Society. On the other hand, "straight" men are not noted for their faithfulness, the restraining factor sometimes being simply the taboo against extra-marital affaires. Perhaps promiscuity is more to do with maleness than homosexuality.

In the past it was common for some gay people to cross dress in a stereotyped role as the submissive partner, while the dominant partner would wear the trousers, another reason for the public view of a transvestite as being gay. The accepted behaviour for men and women in general, is that the woman should be attractive to the man, and that the man should be attracted by the woman. The man should initiate any relationship, he "makes the running", he is the active half. The woman responds, she is passive.

With present day gay couples, the interaction is likely to be much more subtle, focusing on the giving and receiving of mutual pleasure, rather than being goal oriented, as so much heterosexual sex is. The majority of gay people that I have talked with say that they love as man to man. In general, both gay men and lesbians, having 'come out' feel at ease with the way they are, and both have the same feelings about their bodies that most other people have, they certainly wouldn't want to change their sexual organs.

In contrast, many transvestites and transexuals never lose the feeling that they would prefer to be otherwise, either a real man or a real woman, rather than seeing themselves as stuck in the middle. A TV friend of mine, Elaine, who is a very out-going and self-possessed person, who is well used to going out and about and enjoying herself as a man or a woman, in towns and cities all over the world, once said to me, during a conversation, "I wouldn't wish it on my worst enemy!"

Chapter 4
MEN AND WOMEN

The gender paradox! How can someone who is quite definitely male, say that he is wholly or partly female? Many TV's speak of the woman inside them. Many transexuals say that they are women born in the wrong body. Just what differences are there between men and women? The one deciding difference occurs at the moment of conception, in the chromosomes, the coded messages that determine what each cell of our body will be, and how they will specialise. Chromosomes that make someone female are called XX, those that make someone a man are called XY. It would seem that the die is cast, from the biological point of view, at the moment an egg and a sperm join to become a human being. Variations in chromosomes occur, very rarely, but their effect is, as yet, barely understood, in spite of the claims of certain prominent transexuals.

It seems that the foetus begins as female, but, within a few weeks, specialisation occurs in various cells. These, produce hormones, which in turn promote development specifically as male or female. This proceeds through various stages. There is a school of thought that claims the existence of one stage in which the presence of a certain hormone "tells" the foetal brain that it is a boy, otherwise the brain assumes that it is a girl, regardless of other hormones which determine the way the body will develop. Another, more generally accepted theory, is that the male or female hormone "mix", notably the presence of testosterone in the male, accounts for personality differences between the genders, and promotes one or the other gender identity in the foetus.

The trouble is that the professional psychological world is full of pundits all banging the table, promoting their own ideas on what makes a boy, and what makes a girl.

A discussion on BBC's Daytime Live, by a group of specialists, turned into a fairly rowdy debate. We, on the outside, get an over-simplified view, for it is much easier to report some one-line diagnostic pronouncement, than a dissertation on the subtleties that are really involved. I suspect that no one will ever find a definitive answer, for there are too many variables. On one hand, we have the theory that everyone is born with the knowledge of whether he is a boy or a girl. On the other, we have people who say that the differences are all due to upbringing. This is the argument between "nature and nurture". There is, in addition, a school of thought that suggests that all sorts of other features, besides gender attributes, may be inborn. If there really are genetic or chemical characteristics in the foetus that can be manipulated, it raises important ethical questions.

If there is any truth in the idea, that there is some sort of switch that clicks over either before, or just after, a baby is born, the effect it produces must surely be subtle in the extreme. Even if there are hormones that give a tendency to so-called "male" and "female" attributes, between individual men or individual women, both body chemistry and fund-amental emotional make-up can vary widely. In short, can chemistry alone, really tell an infant brain categorically "You are a boy", or "You are a girl"? For a start, it depends on what we mean by masculine and feminine.

Even very young babies seem to be have distinctive person-alities, one may be bright and jolly, another placid, another active. Researchers are fairly clear that a baby, at a point early in its life, acquires the concept of itself as an individual, forming the foundation of the developing personality. But we have a lot to learn about the way this self-image is formed, what it consists of, how and when it is learned, if and how it relates to gender. Other published literature is just as definite in implicating the child's growing environment.

When you sit back and really wonder exactly how much nature needs to provide in the way of gender differences, it comes as a shock to realise how few are really needed. Everything else that we do is learned, learned so thoroughly that we think it is natural, because everyone else behaves the same way.

When it comes to rearing a baby, for every suggestion there is a counter suggestion. It is suggested that, when a mother nurses her baby, she does in the knowledge of its assumed sex, and treats it accordingly, but, surely, it could equally well be said that, in the empathy between mother and baby, she will treat it in the manner which gives maximum comfort. The suggestion is also made that a transvestite is the product of an assertive mother and a meek father. On the other hand, an over aggressive father is sometimes blamed, the idea being that the infant seeks the comfort of its mother, or rejects the father. But lots of children have parents that could fit one or the other description; they don't all appear to become transvestites.

It is sometimes suggested that the TV as a child may have been dressed in excessively feminine clothes, but even young children are well able to express their emotions. If a boy child objected to the way he was dressed, he would probably make sure that he made a mess of his clothes at every opportunity. In any case, nowadays, most clothing for both boys and girls tends to be practical, and not excessively gender related, but there are no fewer TV's. Another suggestion is that the parents discourage mischievous, or adventurous, behaviour too thoroughly. Some TV's blame it on being dressed as a girl, during a game or for a play. But it doesn't affect everyone like that. Interestingly, some sets of twins were interviewed. One might expect that they would have been exposed to the same domestic influences and pressures. But their reaction, in many cases, seemed to be quite individual.

Sometimes groups of transvestites are interviewed about their early lives. Sometimes the transvestites' accounts are compared with those of non-transvestites, as a control. The results tend not to be particularly conclusive, and each person may have a similar experience, but attach different significance to it. All sorts of surveys have been carried out and, while they give food for thought, the samples were necessarily small and the results inconclusive.

It is so easy to blame the parents of a TV. Parents, especially mothers, often go through agonies of guilt and self recrimination, when their son's transvestism becomes known, or they reject it. Yet, if they have done what they thought was right, what else could they do? What is often forgotten is that parents are by no means the only influences on a developing child.

The end product of this growing process may be a boxer, a soldier, an engineer, a doctor, a musician or an artist, attributes of the individual as much as those of the parents or schooling. While an exploration of the past may be useful for an individual to gain an understanding of himself, mere blameplacing is valueless. The aim should be finding a way to plan the present.

I believe that there is simply no one single influence that one can point to as producing a particular personality, or causing gender problems. While one influence may produce a given result from a later experience, in a chain of influence, one soon becomes involved in a chicken and egg situation, trying to decide whether a given situation arises from a certain earlier experience, or whether both are together the result of an even earlier one. When one looks back at life, who can really tell what is cause and what is effect?

In the end, the past is gone and, even if the role one learned so innocently was either too limited, or learned too well, it cannot easily be unlearned.

When I was in my teens there was great interest in the idea that the babies of the future would be born in test tubes as clones, and brought up in creches, so that they would all be identically good and beautiful and healthy.

In fact, later experience with plants, showed that even clones aren't always completely identical to each other, as they grow up. But, in any case, we rejected the idea. We preferred the old, traditional, random way of bringing up children.

The plain fact is that the human personality is immensely complicated. It is the sum of all the random childhood influences and experiences built up, layer by layer. This is what produces the wide ranging variety of humanity that we prize so much.

Chapter 5
OTHER PLACES, OTHER TIMES.

The idea that we may actually be born with a right or wrong gender identity has, of course, been seized on by transexuals and, for that matter, gay people, as a good, acceptable and respectable reason for what they do. Transexuals say that they are "women trapped in a man's body", in other words, that their gender identity is female. Most transvestites and transexuals say that their feelings are something deep within them. It is an attractive idea, which provides a good, solid proof rather than a vague psychological hypothesis. It is a good excuse for us, and a good get-out for Society.

The word identity itself gives a feeling of something concrete, something you could almost put your hand on. If I say my name is Jed, that is my identity, it is firm solid fact. To say that my gender identity is male would seem to be equally concrete; everyone knows what a man is. But do they?

Physically, I look like a man, even when I'm in the bath. But one's personal identity is something much more abstract. It is the feeling of being an individual, the knowledge of one's collection of feelings and emotions, one's place in Society and the world. In the days of the tribe and, later, the small community, it was easy to see oneself as a part of a limited collection of other people and to find one's place in it. Later one had an identity as part of a nation and one of a group of workers. Somehow this contains a concept of one's gender, which has to depend on one's own view of people who look like one's self. If a child learns his gender behaviour from the Society he lives in, then Society defines his concept of masculine and feminine. Each culture's definition has evolved over the centuries in response to the pressures on it. It could be said that it is being unduly influenced in this century by artificial stereotypes promoted by the media. At one time, the cult hero was the shining white knight, gallant but gentle. Now it is Rambo and Dirty Harry.

A study in 1979 compared Sweden and Australia. Both countries were, at that time similar in many ways in terms of population, gross national product, standard of living and so on. Though Sweden was regarded to be much more flexible in its sexual attitudes, Australia recorded seven times more sex change operations.

Other surveys have revealed that as many as 5% of boys and 9.5% of girls, were unhappy with their given sex, during childhood, a far greater proportion than eventually seek the 'sex change'. The figures for adolescent boys was even greater, 30% in Australia, 20% in the USA, contrasted once again with Sweden, where the figure was virtually nil. This throws an interesting light on transexuals, who say that they always, from early childhood, saw themselves as being of the opposite sex. Too much weight should not, perhaps, be given to these figures. It is natural for children to question themselves, and these questions should include gender. Perhaps it is those that don't question, but simply accept, that have difficulties later in life, not necessarily latent transvestism, but also being over-macho or, in the case of women, over feminine.

Perhaps, the baby does have an identity, based on the feelings it is born with, feelings that are far less complicated in concept than we can define, not related to its gender except for a subtle weighting one way or the other. A child spends it life soaking up information, cataloguing it and relating it to previous experience in a manner that is totally and innocently perceptive. Who can say what are the subtleties it experiences? We could suggest that, as it develops a view of itself as a person, it attaches to various attributes that it relates most closely to. Some of the attributes of this personality are imposed on it, but it's interpretation must be based on previous experiences, and feelings, along with this emotional makeup that it has been born with.

From the moment I started questioning myself and those around me, I was intrigued by the relationship between being gay and being transexual or transvestite. What does it mean to be gay? How does it feel? Psychological textbooks have very little to say about TV's and TS's, possibly because they regard us as being an extension of the gay community, or perhaps the writers feel that, subconsciously, we are trying avoid the stigma of homosexuality, which may very well be a part of the truth. But I wonder if, in fact, we are the mirror image of the gay community.

Most gay men are extremely masculine in their everyday demeanour, even though some take a "femme name", and cross dress for parties and so on. At clubs and private functions, some dress in quite startling ways. I have the impression that the reason that gay people find our cross dressing so incomprehensible is that we take it so seriously, and that they see their appearance as an image that they adopt for the occasion. Many gay writings condemn transvestites and transexuals for being pre-occupied with the female stereotype, but for many of us, it goes deeper than that, and we are just as much a product of our beginnings as gay people are. But it would seem that gay people simply do not feel any sort of rigid gender divide, while the transvestite feels its presence very strongly, in that he is in conflict with it. It is ironic that gay groups are campaigning for a modification of this Society's stereotypes, when transvestites and transexuals are the real victims.

For most people, the concept that they adopted in childhood, of the role model, or the degree to which they felt the need to conform to it, was sufficiently flexible to allow them to function peacefully within the limits of what Society, including psychologists, considers to be normal.

Perhaps, if there are early life influences that result in transexualism and transvestism, they may not be so much to do with gender, as a susceptibility to being what we are told we should be. Could we say that a transexual and to a varying, lesser extent, a transvestite is someone in whom the imposed behaviour patterns are so at variance with these predisposing factors, however derived, that there is a stress, which may lie hidden for years. After all, children accept the way they are because they know no different. But other stresses may accumulate and the mind seeks an escape. It may be with the pressures of growing up, or the onset of sexuality. But sometimes it may occur later in life, or in some difficult period. The inference is that, for TV's and TS's, it is to do with relating their "selves" to Society's requirements (which could account for their self-centred nature).

I feel that being gay is also a question of personal identity, and not just a matter of sexuality. One's identity is the view of one's self, but it also includes a concept of relationships with others, according to their gender. We set boundaries between friendship, emotional bonding and sexual feelings, different for people of the same and those of the opposite sex.

Most gay people seem to have a clear idea of their "selves", but it could be suggested that, not attaching strongly to a role model, could lead to not attaching strongly to a relationship model, except that the two seem to develop independently. It also doesn't explain why it seems to be the rule in the gay community that men go with men and women go with women. However, I heard a well known gay man, talking to Radio 1, because of the uproar over his intention to get married, saying, "Just because I'm gay, doesn't mean I can't fall in love with a woman, marry her and have a family."

The issue is confusing, because, of course, people don't fit preconceived patterns, however much they would like to.

Perhaps it could be said that everyone has their own individual combination of self model and relationship model. There are homosexual transvestites, who are attracted to gay or straight men, possibly the same ratio as in the general population. I have two friends who cross dress and see themselves as gay. One sees himself as a transvestite primarily, the other sees himself as being gay primarily.

The situation in other cultures is less easy to determine. The Western taboo about homosexuality is not universal across the world. Some societies, though not acknowledging it publicly, depend on it for stability. While promoting an ideal in terms of behaviour, they accept that the world is less than perfect. In some countries it is formalised and, in addition, a change of role occurs, as with the Xanith of Oman, who are seen by the anthropologist, Wikan, as a "third gender". In several parts of the world, there are men living openly as women. Some are artists in traditional forms of theatre or dance. Others earn a living as male prostitutes, but they may have quite different feelings about themselves.

Since the concepts of being gay or transexual are not really thought of, the situation is difficult to determine, and this applies to historical record as well, since the words had not even been invented. At various times, homosexuality received various degrees of acceptance. In many cultures, including our own, an emotional bond, or love, between two men was often exalted as the purest form of love.

Since ancient times, there have been stories based on male to female changeover, or vice versa. In many religions, various Gods were changed from male to female. Even some Christian saints were transgenderal, while some Hindu Gods are pictured in either gender. There are records of men living as women from both Ancient Jewish and Indian history. In Ancient Greece, there were records by both Hippocrates, the father of medicine and Heredotes, the father of history. The latter gave an account of wholesale male to female changeover in a caucasian tribe. Often, such people would enter the service of the temples, either asexual, or dedicated to the High Priest, the visible manifestation of their God. Or they would become wandering priests.

There is a strong feeling of "not fitting in" with Society, thus such people would disassociate themselves. It is possible that they would become reclusive hermits through the Middle Ages, with the danger of being branded as witches. It is interesting that the stereotypical witch has a large nose and prominent jaw. Also some witches assert that the name for a male witch is not warlock, but witch. The name is not gender specific. Joan of Arc, the heroine of France, was burnt at the stake, but she was first branded a witch, for political reasons, and part of the reasons given was that she invariably wore men's clothes and acted like a man.

There are records, from time to time of people in quite high places who liked to appear, from time to time, in public, as women, from Caligula, through to James I of England, Henri III of France, Edward Hyde, Lord Cornbury, and Maximilian von Lebhorst.

The most well-known, possibly, was Charles Genevieve Chevalier D'Eon de Beaumont, whose name gives rise to one of the names used for transvestism - Eonism, and also for the name of the Beaumont Society. He was a well known, and well-favoured courtier who spied for France in Russia, living as a woman. He continued to do so, when he retired to England, thus retaining his pension from the King of France. He must have been a courageous person, and he was an expert swordsman. While nowadays, he might have been considered transexual, in no way could he be described as a "nancy boy".

But bravery, gallantry, assertiveness and a powerful personality have never been the sole prerogative of the male half of humanity. One has only to consider Boadicea, Joan of Arc, Grace Darling, Florence Nightingale and others like them.

In history, it was fairly common for women to live as men to obtain work. In the Netherlands around 100 court cases were reported in the 17th. and 18th. Century of women who joined the army or worked as sailors in a male role. While they would not have considered themselves as being men, for the concept of transexuality had not arisen, many of them considered themselves "as good as any man" and a part of male Society. Some suffragettes, who were trying to break out of the female stereotype, sometimes went to excess in the wearing of male clothes. Among them was George Sand, the first woman allowed to wear male clothes by Presidential decree.

What differences were there between those days and now? The fashions at court for both men and women were ornate, and there was much greater freedom to express oneself. Dress is, after all, a personal statement. While any form of extreme social deviation was proscribed, in private it may not have been considered remarkable. Written records were sparse and had little to say about ordinary people. Certainly there was much more space, with people living in widely separated small communities. Women and men stayed together and worked together, in the farms and little village workshops. There wasn't the separation between the men "going out" to work and the women "staying at home". How much difference this would make, I don't know. One could visualise a father saying of one of his sons, "The lad's a bit soft", or "a bit fey" but, so long as the work was done, perhaps little more would be said.

Society changed drastically with the beginning of the Industrial Revolution, with people crowded into worker's terraces in large cities. There was less space to get away and be oneself, everyone overlooked each other. Ordinary people possibly became more judgmental. The structure of war changed too. Previously, they had directly involved relatively small numbers of the population, often mercenaries, or professionals, who were presumably "cut out" for the job. As larger and larger armies evolved, they became more and depersonalised with more and more mechanisation. More importantly, there was a need to breed large numbers of men for conscripts, machine minders in factories and labourers in the mines and the constructional projects. It wasn't entirely successful; at the end of the day many would turn to booze and fighting to escape from the futility of it all. Who was it said "Give me a six year old boy and I'll make you a soldier"?

People's social behaviour became more rigid and isolated emotionally. The image of the Victorian father, in the middle and upper classes is of a stiff, stern person, keeping himself remote from his family, something of a lonely figure. In the last forty years, people seem more and more as small cogs in a giant machine. A serious problem, when people come "under care", with the sheer size of the large schools and hospitals and other statutory bodies, even for those working for a large company, is the establishment, or maintenance, of a sense of personal identity.

At the same time, with the development of films and television, people were presented with artificial stereotypes, and tended to identify with them. Many people try to be what they would like to be, rather than what they are. They also try to impose these behaviour patterns on others. The growth of the newspapers meant that there were less secrets. Since the only really visible transvestites, in the early part of this century, were the gay "queens" the psychologists of the day labelled them as sexual perverts, along with homosexuals. So it was hardly surprising that the general public took the same attitude. In the last few decades, the professional attitude to gay people has changed, but a similar change in relation to transvestism has not occurred to any great degree.

Transvestism seems to be associated in people's minds with decadent cultures, from the Rome of Caligula's day through to Berlin between the wars. In such societies, which were, to an extent, tolerant, those people that were hidden may have felt more able to come into the open. But it is true to say that more notice would be taken of such societies than, say, a small group in Balham. But, in any case, the words transvestite and transexual had not been invented. The coming of the scientific era produced a preoccupation with sorting, classifying and labelling. There was a spread of scientific pursuits as ordinary people began to study science and engineering, and people were labelled in ways other than their nationality or religion.

The first medical description of transexualism was by Esquirol in 1838, while Krafft-Ebing, in 1869, considered transvestism to be related to effeminate homosexuality. In 1870, Westphal published a work dealing with the subject. Havelock Ellis coined the name Eonism and the name Transvestism was invented by Magnus Hirsch in 1910, the first person to describe it as a heterosexual phenomenon.

It would appear that, through all this period, there was a preoccupation with sexual direction and sexuality, and only during the thirties did the first ideas of transexuality and gender disorientation begin to appear. In fact, the first gender reassignment surgery took place in 1930, of the Danish artist Einar Wegener who became Lily Elbe, though it attracted little attention, the World's attention being centred on the events in Germany which culminated in World War II. It was the endocrinologist, Harry Benjamin, who recognised transexuality as a syndrome in 1953, while the Professor of psychology at

Harvard University, at that time, John Money, coined the term Gender, as in Gender Identity and Gender Role.

It is a characteristic of humankind that, when we study a subject, we divide it into categories. We do the same thing with people. We put them into pigeonholes and label them. We reward or punish them accordingly. But nature is not so tidy; people don't fit neatly into pigeon holes.

Four years ago - it seems a long time now - I applied to be sponsored as a member of the Beaumont Society. A meeting was arranged at 9 o'clock one Sunday evening, at Nottingham railway station, with a person who took me to a gay bar nearby. I was nervous enough, since it was the first time I'd been in a gay pub, and, being nearly empty, my hoarse whisper seemed to carry to all four corners. When I was asked if I wore a nightie to bed (I wear pyjamas) I wanted to fade away. Towards the end of the conversation, he said "Oh! You're a fetishist then!"

That simple remark set me on a voyage of discovery. The aim of this book is to try and show that there is no clear division between one kind of person and another.

I found much the same attitude at the meetings I attended. Either you were transexual or you were a fetishist. I didn't feel that I was just one or the other and it caused me to look at myself, not just in relation to the whole transvestite community, but Society as well.

I am not a label. I am a person.

Chapter 6
GROWING UP

Throughout the whole TV community is a thousand different life experiences. The danger is, that we construct a stereotyped scenario, like the account of the onset, progress and remission of someone suffering from measles. Everybody in the world is different and so is every TV. Most TV's reading this will identify with some of my suggestions, but be violently opposed to others.

The actual situation varies with each transvestite. Not all will go through a phase of wanting to "change sex", and few start to look for a male partner, for instance. Those that have 'come out' say simply "I just like to wear women's clothes sometimes" and leave it at that. Most "know" somehow that it has always been with them, although many say they can point to an event in their lives that acted as a trigger.

A friend of mine tells the story about of his father buying an old wardrobe, cleaning it and varnishing it as a present for my friend's sister. My friend doesn't ever remember being jealous of his sister, or ever wanting to play with dolls or join in any other little girl's games. As far as he knew, he was just an ordinary child, living in a happy, well balanced family. But somehow the wardrobe, and its contents, attracted his interest.

I remember when I was four years old, I went with my mother to visit a friend of hers who had a daughter about my age. Suddenly she appeared in the doorway of the room where we were and said "Mum! Where's my liberty bodice?"

I was fascinated by words, even at that age. I used to sit on my Dad's knee and try to pick out words in the Daily Telegraph. I had heard of liberty boats, but didn't really know what they were. So in all innocence, I piped up "What's a liberty bodice?" I can still remember the shocked silence in the room, then the little girl was quickly shoo'ed away.

In those days women's undergarments were never mentioned. They certainly weren't openly advertised, as they are now, apart from the local Spirella corsetiere. I suppose this may have triggered my interest, though I didn't start to dress until much later, due to lack of opportunity. In fact, I thought little more of it, or of girls. I never really came across any, for I had very little contact with children, of either sex, of my own age. I would see girls pass by just as one would see a policeman, a postman or any kind of person. They just were.

Nursery nurses will tell you that, in a group dressing up game, there is usually at least one little boy that will head for the girl's clothes. It may be that he is experimenting with gender differences by role play. Probably, he will, in the end, be quite happy to be a boy. Most children play dressing up games; often little boys will try on their sister's or mother's clothes, then go off for a game of football and forget all about it.

But, for some others, it fills a deeper need. Perhaps the mind says "I can't take this", and it is a release. It may be that the little boy's real self contains components that cannot be reconciled with the concept of manhood that is being presented to him. In most cases, he doesn't consciously realise this and, usually, he realises that it is something that is frowned on, so he dresses in secret and doesn't tell anybody.

There is one feature of growing up, for a boy, that is clearly observable and within all men's experience. On growing towards being a man, he suppresses those aspects of his personality that he perceives as unmanly, defined by his experience of the culture he lives in. He needs to be "one of the gang". If these parts of him are, in fact, important features of that personality, they are going to surface from time to time.

On joining school, a boy may be a little "different", something soon sensed by the other children, and their reaction can exacerbate the situation. Thus it may be that, for those that grow up in a supportive peer group, it may be less of a problem. Otherwise, he may react by withdrawing into himself, or he may become excessively aggressive. It cannot be automatically assumed, of course, that the shy boy who keeps to himself, or the school bully, are potential transvestites. In any case, most transvestites report a perfectly normal school life.

Over the whole scenario, there is tremendous variation. Many TV's start dressing in childhood, many others start in puberty, but there are some who may suddenly find comfort in dressing much later in life. Most TV's, however, seem to start around the age of 7 or 8, when it could be said that the pressure to "be a man" begins.

While the exploration of sexuality, as opposed to behaviour patterns, may begin in childhood, it begins in earnest in teenage. All that one has learnt about one's self and one's relationships, and the sum of one's experience, is reviewed in relation to this new factor in one's life. But the pressure to conform and to project a masculine image also rises greatly. Thus, at a time when the boy is already a mass of emotions, he may have the feeling of being at one with women, conflicting with the idea that he is slipping from the pedestal of manhood, and it can with some TV's, produce particular problems.

Popular books on transvestism and transexualism deal with it only as a social phenomenon. Transvestite organisations traditionally deny that sexuality is a feature of cross-dressing, or fudge the issue. But why should we have such negative feelings towards something that is a perfectly natural function, and a vital part of our lives?

What I have to say next, may be controversial, but if we started looking at sexual issues in a mature manner, instead of trying to pretend they don't exist, perhaps we could help people before they got into trouble. But let me make it clear that I am in no way associating myself with those who preach sexual freedom, when what they really mean is sexual anarchy.

In his book "The Naked Ape", Dr. Desmond Morris, says of human beings "This unusual and highly successful species spends a great deal of time examining his higher motives and an equal amount of time studiously ignoring his fundamental ones." How is it, of all the animal kingdom, human beings bring the most bizarre rituals into what is, after all, only a natural process?

Dr. Morris describes early human existence as being in small tribes of people, living in the forest, moving from place to place, eating from the fruit and vegetation which was ready to hand. There was an emotional bond between the various members of the tribe, which was expressed in caresses, mutual grooming and so on. A change in the world's climate forced the tribes to move, more and more, out into the open and, with a reduction in the availability of a vegetable diet, over thousands of years, there was a shift towards meat eating and hunting. Thus parties of males would range far and wide in search of food. Their inventiveness in the production of weapons made them more successful and allowed them to compete with the specialist carnivores that had been provided with the optimum equipment by nature. Meanwhile the females remained together, rearing the young. Thus the male "gang" developed, and a greater separation between male and female societies came about.

The most successful hunters were the most resourceful and a new larger brain evolved. The increased learning period and longer maturation of the young meant that they had to be cared for over a longer period. To facilitate this, the pair bond formed within the tribal group, what psychologists call a dyadic relationship.

There is not space here to describe Dr. Morris's argument fully, but the result was a greatly increased complexity in the human social structure, with tribal groups, but a division between different couples. This complexity increased even more as man developed a pastoral society, which he had to defend along with his continuing foraging expeditions. The tribal group lost a great deal of its mobility. Man also used his inventiveness to increase the complexity of his Society even more, with competition and power struggles.

The social structure in which we live, has evolved and has been patched together and modified over thousands of years to support changing circumstances. Monogamous relationships, and limitation of homosexuality, concentrated on the family unit, and allowed for the extended rearing of children. Whatever our animal instincts, they are controlled in the civilisation we have built for ourselves. We talk about unnatural sexual practices, but it could be said that all present day sex is unnatural. We control it for many good practical reasons, but we still have our animal urges. There is, however, a difference between suppression and control, and, as we control our sexual drives, the mind releases the stress so produced in the form of fantasies, often extremely bizarre.

A feature of the tribal unit with which I started this chapter was the emotional bond between the members of the tribe. In this increasingly isolationist society, we no longer fulfil our emotional needs by physical contact, except on rare occasions.

Dr.Morris suggests that, as tribes grew into nations, larger and more densely populated, the system collapsed, breaking up into family groups. With the Industrial Revolution, the village community disappeared and large anonymous towns and cities developed. Thus people became more isolated, coming together into short term, transient "tribes", the groups and societies, spectator events, sports and other clubs and so on. Emotional communication is formalised in such groups, and in other ways. We are all very aware of keeping a "personal space" around us.

The events and influences through childhood may leave us with emotional needs that are unfulfilled, or with some that are particularly strong. Strong emotions of any kind, even fear, can give rise to release in sexual expression. It is important to realise that fantasies don't come from nowhere. While they may spring from some experience both dramatic and sexual, it may be this is just the trigger or focus. Everyone builds up a picture of their "ideal" love affair, in the form of a story, which is modified and added to, as the years go by. It is a powerful and important part of life, motivating and yet releasing stress. Even if erotic in the final outcome, the fantasy will be fashioned out of all one's past, as well as present, emotional needs. It may re-enact painful episodes in one's life, often in an allegorical form, if the source of the pain cannot be confronted. The aim is a satisfactory outcome, in which there may be an attempt at mastery of the emotional problem. If, for someone, these emotional needs are not being met in daily life, perhaps because of some impediment in expressing them, or if mastery is not achieved, is it possible that a fantasy can get out of control? If the fantasy becomes such an important part of someone's life that it starts to get confused with reality, then the dream that something can happen, can turn into the belief that it will happen.

I wonder if we will ever become a mature enough society, to be able to exercise our fantasies, without them getting out of hand and destabilising our daily lives, or causing harm or hurt to others. Human beings don't seem to be able to approach any function in moderation. They either suppress it or go over the top. One day, perhaps, there will be no shame for someone, whose fantasies could result in harm or hurt to another, from seeking help. By that time, perhaps, counselling techniques, in all their variety, will have come of age to assist, or replace, the more direct therapies used nowadays.

Many people have negative attitudes to fetishism, but many, many others put their fantasies into practice, in a wholly innocent way. Perhaps the trick is to use fantasies, rather than just having them, but they enjoy experimenting with the senses, in the wearing of explicit clothes and exciting fabrics, or experiencing emotions of fear, pain, helplessness, dominance and submission, in a safe and loving environment. They see it as a more adventurous way of expressing themselves sexually, without it becoming an obsession, or letting it become the only way that they can be stimulated.

Chapter 7
FANTASY

There are books and magazines devoted to the erotic side of transvestism as a branch of the sex industry, ranging from contact magazines, where people can advertise for partners, to the picture books, usually smuggled from abroad, featuring "she-males".

Many people, of course, enjoy the "forbidden fruit" aspect, which they see as their "secret vice" or "wicked sin". For them to confess, or to "come out" would de-mystify the ritual and destroy the excitement. But there are many others who have feelings of guilt after the event, or are frightened that someone will find out. Often the excitement is increased by a danger element, or deliberate risk, as with the pantie thief. It must be pointed out, though, that many TV's have stolen their first set of underclothes, simply because they felt unable to obtain them any other way.

Yet there is, for some, a sexual fillip in the thought that the clothing has actually belonged to a woman. Often, fetishists will imagine a woman, not necessarily one that they know, usually young and pretty, and imagine themselves in her mind and body. Thus, for some, there may be a special significance in clothes that have belonged to a woman, in that they feel closer to her, taking on her attributes. On a more innocent level, the lover who keeps a lock of hair from the loved one, does not simply have a keepsake, but a token of his, or her, life force.

So I feel that it is reasonable to suggest that someone who might be called gender shifted, in other words, not entirely at ease with the male role, possibly due to an unrealistic view of what is required, might have fantasies relating to cross-dressing. The daydream may range from enjoyment of unusual and unfamiliar clothes and materials (women's clothing, in any case having sexual connotations), with the urge for personal adornment, common to all human beings, through the idea of experiencing the "mysteries of womanhood", to adopting a role that is perceived to be less demanding.

In fact, as many motives have been proposed as there have been writers on the subject. Total dressing has been referred to as the 'whole girl' fetish. Many transvestites never progress beyond underclothes. Indeed, there is a magazine devoted to photographs of such TV's. From dressing in front of a mirror, they progress to taking photographs of themselves, then can see them in print. Other TV's enjoy looking at such photos. It is necessarily a lonely occupation, and they often advertise in contact magazines for others with the same interest. They may have fantasies about going out in public, so that others can see them. Once again fantasy is one thing, reality is quite another.

Some years ago, a man, on several occasions, exposed himself to women, when dressed in female underwear. The police caught up with him and he appeared in the magistrate's court, where he was described as a shy, inoffensive man, who had few friends and kept to himself at work. Although the magistrate's judgment was lenient and reasonable, he became a pariah in the neighbourhood where he lived and had to move.

Transvestites and transexuals usually disassociate themselves from any suggestion of either fetishism, or bisexual feelings. They deny that there is any erotic or sexual motive in their dressing. They are not lying, or even, in most cases, hiding from themselves. It is the interplay between gender motives and sexual expression and preference that creates such a bewildering complexity to the whole subject. But, for many

TV's, at some time or another, it is a powerful erotic experience.

In the single transvestite, fantasies turn towards female dress, or being a woman. Release occurs with more day-to-day "realistic" dressing rather than exotic fabrics, leather, latex etc. And the lonely TV may meet his emotional needs by constructing his own female partner. The majority of transvestites are heterosexual and remain so, being content with a solitary, auto-erotic ritual, between the TV's male and female self, as it were.

Many transvestites are cross dressers and no more. They never lose sight of the fact that they are a man. For most there is a powerful auto-erotic motivation, especially through the sexually charged teenage years. One might expect the TV to go on to other fetishistic rituals as the novelty of dressing wears off, but, for many, familiarity does not lead to further excesses, and does not reduce the need, though it may modify it. For some, the fetish either develops into a desire to imitate the whole woman or the erotic element seems to decrease as they develop a female "other self".

For some, the knowledge, barely comprehended, that they have not just dressed as a woman, but, in their minds, they have been a woman, seems create guilt feelings greater than if it were just a sexual release. The idea that they have negated all the effort put into being a man may produce deep emotional distress.

The fantasy may be extended to imagining a lesbian partner. Often the TV is "caught in the act" or there is an element of coercion in the fantasy. In the fantasy he may begin by resisting, but finish by enjoying it, as if the TV is telling himself that it is not really his fault. A reflection of these fantasies can be seen in the advertisements for the telephone sex lines. Titles, like "Forced into Petticoats" and "Blackmailed into Femininity", may not be masochistic so much as a defence against guilt. On the other hand, some men become women in their minds, with reversed sexual fantasies as an extension of the dressing and on the purely physical plane, which they would never dream of putting into practice.

For some others, there may be an unconscious emotional attraction to men. Because they are women in their minds, they are still heterosexual. The trouble is that some people label themselves too rigidly as heterosexual or homosexual, and it can give rise to an amount of internal confusion. In accepting this, but acknowledging that their real sexual turn on is women, they can explore these emotions, by experimenting in the mind through the medium of fantasy, without hurting themselves, so long as they recognise the boundary with reality.

Again, if a TV advertises in a contact magazine, his "partner in dressing" may want things for which he is unprepared, such as mutual masturbation or more. For some TV's, it is simply an extension of the fantasy, in pursuit of greater realism, or they may be, unconsciously, confronting past hurtful feelings in relationships, while others may have genuine homosexual, or bisexual, preferences and seek to explore this side of their nature by meeting other TV's. The main thing is for no-one to be hurt, emotionally or physically.

Perhaps the trouble is, that we see the sexual urge as distinct from the culmination of a loving relationship, and concentrate on sexual images rather than people. Perhaps the rule should be: Only have sex with someone you like. In human terms, perhaps, the sexual act is meaningless by itself and, if pursued as an extension of a fantasy, it can simply add more problems, or lead to an endless chasing of more and more extended fantasies, if the emotional needs behind the fantasy are not addressed.

The preceding chapters may have been heavy going for my more straight laced readers, but they illustrate the complicated ways in which people's minds try to align their emotional, sexual and relational needs with the needs of Society as a whole. These emotional binds are real; they need to be acknowledged and not swept under the carpet.

The negative attitudes we have, mean that sex is something we don't talk about, which means that we don't discuss the problems either. AIDS, which is highly contagious to hetero-sexual men and women, as well as bisexual and homosexual people, has forced us to confront the issues. In addition, there is an increasing awareness that most sexually transmitted diseases, some of which cause little trouble for men, are extremely dangerous for women. One of the reasons is, of course, that the male organs are on the outside, while the female ones are internal, so that early symptoms may go unnoticed. But also, Society and professional attitudes are quite different for "men's problems" and "women's problems".

The relationship of identification to fetishism seems to be different for different TV's. Sometimes it follows on, sometimes it seems to arise independently. For some the "dressing" is primarily fetishistic and, in extending the sexual script, and keeping it alive, the TV may go on to enactments of, for example, female domination. For some TV's, it is never part of the sexual script, for others it is a part of it in their teenage, while for some others it becomes a part as they get older. Some TV's are sexually fulfilled and still find a need to cross dress, while some can separate the fetish from the cross-dressing and redirect their sexuality in another direction. It may be that the need for fetishism is the same as for anyone else, maybe a need for a more active sexual role. Many women enjoy fetishism, though, it is said, rarely involving cross-gender fantasies. Is it possible that the fetishism is a feature of the person, with the cross gender aspect being an expression of the "feministic" urge?

The negative feelings we have towards the sexual, auto-erotic side of transvestism means that it carries its own weight of guilt. Typically, after any fetishistic session, of any kind, there is a feeling of self-disgust, similar to the post-coital depression that some men suffer. One might also visualise a TV setting out one evening to relax as a woman, with sexual feelings aroused that, at that time are not wanted. He may well, in time, want to get rid of this source of annoyance. Many TV's have the wish to relate to women as friends and companions, without the "intrusion" of sexual feelings. There can arise an urge to experience this internal woman separately from the sexual experience. In rejecting a part of the sexual script, it may become incoherent, which may lead the TV to reject the whole.

Though few established transvestites say much about their early days or their private lives, some, that are living on their own, will admit to the need for some sexual release. In fact, some will admit to having a collection of more exotic clothes for wear at home, in addition to their normal 'going out' clothes. I was talking to a charming, graceful and impeccably turned-out TV one evening at a meeting, when she said "I have two wardrobes, you know".

Here we have an important point. The transvestite on his own may have the same sexual need as anyone, yet have a different need to be a social woman. Thus his dressing tends to polarise. Such a TV resolves his sexual and gender dressing by having two sets of clothes, and dresses according to the purpose of the moment. Sometimes he will dress for fetishistic reasons. Sometimes he is content to spend a period "being a woman".

Chapter 8
THE TRANSVESTITE

A childhood TV may start by trying on a dress and suddenly he is a new, exciting person. A TV starting in the sexually charged teens may start with underclothing. If the dressing was part of a sexual fantasy, one would expect the clothes to be taken off afterwards, with some disgust, until the next time, but in the TV there develops a wish to stay in the female clothes. The aim becomes the exploration of another part of himself, rather than sensual stimulation, and the preference becomes for more everyday female wear, progressing from underclothing through to outer clothes and makeup. The TV buys a wig and displays extreme ingenuity in constructing false bosoms.

The favourite seems to be old socks or stockings filled with birdseed. I once experimented with lentils which are flat and smooth. Unfortunately I had a leak and spent weeks finding orange specks on the royal blue bedroom carpet. Some TV's use heavy duty carnival balloons filled with wallpaper paste. A leak in one of these is uncomfortable to say the least. One TV told me that he had left a pair in the back of his wardrobe and forgotten them. They went bad and he spent days looking for the source of a peculiar smell that was drifting around his house.

Affluent TV's can buy the silicone prostheses that are made for women that have lost their natural breasts through surgery. A surprising number of TV's have beards or moustaches, which they disguise with great ingenuity. Most TV's pad their hips in some way. Alternatively, they wear a loose jacket, or a dress with a peplum waist. I take the latter course. I hate hip pads, so I tell myself that some of the most beautiful women in the world have figures like greyhounds. A TV can buy special under garments to strap his male bits and pieces out of sight, or wear a pantie girdle. A friend of ours tells us he uses cling film, which has given us cause for a deal of speculation. The most comfortable solution is not to wear a tight skirt!

Many of my readers will have seen the film "Tootsie", though the character was not a transvestite as such. Dustin Hoffman also had the opportunity for a retake if he got something wrong, though that is not to take away the brilliance with which he showed how a man can portray a woman.

Men rarely feel the wind against their legs, except when they wear shorts, and it is not the same as the swishing of a dress against the legs, nylon clad, with high heels. Where does sexuality start and sensuality finish? When a man puts on an evening clothes, or a woman a ballgown, it may not seem to give rise to sexual feelings and it is a means to an end, that is, for a special occasion or to go out for an evening for a special person, yet the dressing up itself gives a frisson of excitement.

I once wrote in the Beaumont Bulletin, "We can forget being a pompous, reserved, shy, inhibited man (Strike out as inapplicable). We can exercise our intellect and our senses and express ourselves in a new way. We can escape for a while. This is what recreation is all about."

Helplines frequently receive calls from TV's, who tell the operator that they are dressed and saying how happy they feel. They say, "I've never felt so feminine!". They are exploring a whole new world of the mind. It is not, of course, the everyday world of a woman, but one that she could enter if she chose, yet a man cannot.

Many TV's are people that simply cross-dress and no more, with thought neither for sexual excitement nor for becoming transexual. They simply find enjoyment in experimenting with clothes and fabrics and accessories. Men have four modes of dress: casual (jeans and sweatshirt), casual (sports jacket and flannels), formal (suit and tie), ultra formal (evening dress or morning suit). The divisions are strict and the variation that is allowed is very limited. So, some find an outlet for their urge to experiment with dress by becoming TV's.

What also happens is that the transvestite finds great peace and relaxation when dressed. He finds simple pleasure in dressing for its own sake and, given the chance, will live the female role for days at a time.

Some TV's like to spend all day pottering around the house, wearing ordinary jeans and a jumper, except that the jumper has a size 18 label, instead of chest 36. The clothes, in effect, are just the outward image of the feminine entity the TV is trying to express.

Brierley, in his book "Transvestism", spoke of transexuals being born with a male body but a female identity. He put forward the idea that the transvestite has a bi-polar identity, switching from one to the other. Certainly transvestites switch roles, but does their self-image also change?

Occasionally, you meet TV's who say that they feel as if they are two people in the same body and, often, they are in a state of considerable frustration. I am not talking about Multiple Personality Disorder, which is a different thing and is usually accompanied by other symptoms. These TV's are firmly based in reality and say things like "I want to stop this urge to dress up. I'm fed up with being two different people", but perhaps it was some of these people that found their way to Dr.Brierley's office.

I must go back to the idea that identity is not something concrete. Somebody may see himself as a man, but what kind of a man? One explanation goes as follows: Central to everybody's existence is their view of themselves as a person, a unique self. This central self has concepts embodied in a series of sub-selves - as a man, as a father, as a tradesman and so on. Each is linked to the others and to the central self in a balanced system. These, and the interactions between them, are modified and refined day by day, to take account of new experiences and emotions.

If one perceives certain features of one's self that can't be fitted into the sub-self labelled "man", one might feel it necessary to express them in one's lifestyle, building up a new sub-self, which, in time, may be labelled "woman". Over a period, a fund of experience is built up, and feedback is obtained from one's feelings and the reactions of others. The new sub-self complements the male sub-self, but is subordinate to it, and a balanced self-system is restored.

In the people mentioned above, the two sub-selves had, perhaps, been allowed to develop within their total self structure in such a way that they were conflicting. The majority of TV's are perfectly certain about the relative importance of the two sub-selves in their lives. I think most TV's are quite clear about being one person, but feel that they cannot express their personality to the full in the male role only. A psychologist may say that "regular dressing has the effect of weakening the masculine identity". Using the same terminology, a TV might say that it is a response to an identity that is not particularly masculine to start with, or that he is more in tune with his real self. Indeed, the established TV may be all the more secure in his identity from having taken the opportunity to experiment.

Not all TV's go as far as this, of course. Some say "I don't dress to be a woman. I simply dress the way I feel." Some say they want to express the femininity within them; others say they feel that their personality is to an extent feminine. Others simply take a rest from being a man. At one end of the scale, there are transvestites who simply enjoy dressing, not necessarily as a sexual fillip, but they may enjoy this aspect as well. They may have "come out" early and accepted non-conformity easily. At the other end, there are TV's for whom the idea of themselves as partly feminine is important. They may have been dressing in secret for a much longer period.

Books by transvestites describe the feelings and motivations with a poetry that I don't possess. One can say that a TV wishes, for that short while, gentleness instead of assertiveness, prettiness instead of handsomeness, emotionality, sensitivity, playfulness, gracefulness, peacefulness, compassion and the enjoyment of colour, design and beauty in a way that he feels that he cannot as a man. Just as a woman may put on jeans and a jumper to work in the garden as the clothing for the job, or, if she is a female executive, "power-dresses" to perform her work, so the TV uses the dress, the makeup and dainty shoes, to bring his hidden side to life.

For most of the time, the transvestite leads a perfectly normal male life, and the urge to cross dress occurs at irregular intervals, sometimes as a relief from stress at work. Indeed, though he may not, in some cases, accept it, his male part is as important to him as the chance to escape from it for a while.

It could be said that transvestites are rebelling, albeit unconsciously, against a convention that they cannot perfectly adapt to. Not only that, but that it is meeting some inner need and the identification carries on into daily life. Many TV's wear some item of female clothing underneath their male clothes and it gives them a feeling of comfort. A great many paint their toenails. Indeed, the greater the disapprobation that is perceived, the greater is the urge, the need to "break out". That is why the guilt is so destructive, the suppression so counter-productive.

Some TV's are outgoing and forceful, even in their female role. Others are quieter and more withdrawn. The motivation for some is largely erotic, others are more nearly transexual.

The variation is endless and the same goes for their attitude to dressing. There seems to be no common family, or childhood, background. It affects every walk of life from the lowest to the highest in the land; engineers, lorry drivers, drill sergeants, judges, company directors and office cleaners.

Many TV's are high achievers in their male role. It may be that, in having to work so much harder to be a man, they are better at it. It might seem odd to suggest that to wear a dress is a good way to become a company director, but it occurs to me that, if they have come to terms with their transvestism, they may, in finding occasional release from the problems of being a man, be able to approach them more positively.

The average transvestite is normally indistinguishable from any other man; he doesn't appear in the slightest effeminate. A voice on the helpline might say, "I'm 53, I weigh 14 stone, I drive a Scania truck, and I'm shaking like a leaf. I did a tour in Cyprus in the army and telephoning you is the most frightening thing I've ever done."

This is why it comes as such a shock when a TV "comes out" and admits what he is. If I have talked about the work I am doing, people ask "How did you get into that then?" and look amazed when I say "Well, I am one".

Some time ago, I heard women discussing men and one suggested that "men, in general, are frightened of women" and, since then, I have heard young men on the radio, saying the same thing. In order to function in this society, men have to build an appearance of self-confidence, which can be quite fragile. For a man to ask a girl to go out with him is an act of courage, for refusal will shatter this facade. Further, in not being able to acknowledge feelings, the effect of strong attraction to a girl may itself be demoralising. In groups, some men combat these feelings by wolf whistles, and competing in tall stories of their prowess or the chance of a conquest.

Many TV's are extremely successful in attracting girlfriends. Without knowing it, they may be approaching the girl as a friend, rather than just a potential lover. Even though she knows nothing of his secret occupation, she senses an empathy which gives him an added attraction. On the other hand, some TV's may not be able to sustain a lasting relationship. Somewhere, I read that TV's are in love with all women, and cannot fall in love with any one. It all hangs on the definition of being "in love", of course. The TV feels an empathy with all women, but that is not the same as being in love with them. But, in seeing all women as potential friends, some may have difficulty in settling on one lover.

Many others, though, are shy and introverted. Perhaps they are unable to communicate with women, so to an extent they build themselves a woman with whom they can relate. Somewhere else I read that a transvestite is in love with himself. This view is reinforced by the introspective nature of many TV's, having grown up, to an extent isolated from society. It also springs from the idea of the closet TV admiring himself in front of a mirror. If the TV is too shy, or has some emotional impediment to free communication, he is not going to be able to find a partner, so it fills an emotional need as well.

I talked about the idea that all the things we do, and all our "natural" behaviour patterns, are learned throughout our childhood. To an extent, these include a whole variety of signals and responses, often too subtle to define, as subtle as the feelings that are being transmitted. Whole books are written on "body language", yet the very act of describing them debases them. We give signals to people and look for an expected response; similarly other people look for the expected response from us.

If we respond in the wrong way, to someone who gives a signal, we give him, or her, a sense of unease. One form of shyness is a lack of confidence that one can give the right responses in a given environment. One can be a famous comedian, or a chart-topping pop singer, yet be painfully shy in private life. One can be a confident worker, handling every task with ease and panache, yet, at a party or a dance, be the eternal wallflower.

In male to female communication, a whole subtle range of ways of behaving are expected. If one has not built up a fund of experience with girls, then one can put out the wrong signals. Perhaps the shy TV involuntarily puts out feminine ones. A few months ago a girl at work called me "a weird man", completely out of the blue, as far as I could tell. When I was about four, a girl said to me "You're as soft as grease!". It took me forty years to work out what she meant.

Many shy people feel that every effort to express themselves, either as individuals or as men, meets a rebuff. Life always seems to have a banana-skin ready for them. A shy man often cannot overcome that barrier to asking a woman to go out with him, so sidesteps it with friendly conversation.

There is a second kind of shyness, much deeper and much more difficult to tackle. I could perhaps call it an emotional block. Possibly, most men suffer from it, to an extent. They have been conditioned for so many years into the "stiff upper lip" attitude, to be self-sufficient and independent. Someone who has, for year after year, been "put down" and rejected, will have enclosed his emotions in layers of "don't care" to spare himself hurt. When the time comes that he needs to express feelings or emotion, he finds he cannot do so. He might be quite outgoing, and well able to communicate at a distance, but, as soon as someone comes close, he will withdraw emotionally, or even tense or flinch when touched.

It would seem that the best policy for many TV's is to put aside the idea that their cross-dressing is a problem to them, and get on with the business of a positive approach to life.

Chapter 9
THE SECRET CONFLICT

Teenage is often a period of confusion and frustration, as the adulthood, that was a perceived future in childhood, is fast becoming a reality. There are new feelings to take on board, and new pressures. Learning becomes more intensive and goal-oriented, yet there are doubts as to whether the goal is the right one, as the teenager is invited to make a once-and-for-all choice about his career, and hence his future life. There is the testing of new relationships with adults, particularly parents, and movements towards independence as an individual. Suddenly letters arrive marked "Mr." instead of "Master". Hopes for success are accompanied by fears of failure. One's relationship to one's own and the other gender take on new meanings. There is much exaggerated posing, until an acceptable gender behaviour is found.

Generally, throughout the teens and twenties, sessions of cross-dressing are intermittent, but the need to cross-dress often feels like taking two steps forward and one back. Some teenage transvestites experience great confusion, even a sense of unreality, as they try to relate themselves to the world that they find themselves entering. Generally, the masculine side is uppermost as they set out to build a career. Some build the two identities very quickly and accept the female role as a release. Others "hold in" their feelings, without identifying them, for half a lifetime. Yet others continue to fight their cross-dressing and may never lose the feelings of guilt. Sometimes they have difficulties in developing their male role, either becoming repressed or over-compensating, sometimes developing negative feelings towards their manhood.

With most men, as middle age approaches, the need for an aggressive approach to a career lessens, one's lifestyle becomes more mellow and one starts to relax from the masculine stance. It is normal for most men to adopt a less extreme masculine role as they become grandfathers rather than fathers. The attitude to life softens, one no longer needs the macho image to survive, and the duality reasserts itself. In addition, the normal worries and stresses of daily life will add to the need for an escape. So, cross-dressing may occur more often. There is often the feeling that transvestism has a weakening effect on one's sex life, but this could be simply the natural effect of advancing years.

While it is sometimes suggested that there is a male equivalent of the female menopause, it isn't marked by the same obvious physical changes. There is a general slowing down and, while most men are physically capable of sex into their eighties, there tends to be a reduction in drive. Whether this is a physical or emotional change is a matter of conjecture. Probably it is a combination of both. The forties are when many men take stock; they reassess their lives. The children are growing up and leaving home, they may have advanced as far as they might reasonably expect in their trade or profession. Possibly they are no longer as able, or willing, to work as hard, or sustain the stress as in former years. There is time to look around and, perhaps, wonder what they have achieved that is worthwhile and how much time there is left. For some men, the reappraisal is far-reaching, and the solution drastic, causing them to discard an outwardly highly successful career, to start in a completely new direction. On the other hand, feelings that have been submerged for years may surface.

There is, often, a deeper confidence in oneself as a person, less need for other's good opinion, which may be a reason why TV's seem to 'come out' in their forties. The proportion of middle-aged members in the Beaumont Society, for instance, is quite high.

For those that stay in the closet, the feeling of identification of themselves as women, and the idea of "not being quite a man", produces the deepest feelings of guilt. It is this society's most awful sin. Some secret TV's are literally paranoic about discovery and go to the most amazing lengths to hide their activities from even their closest relatives. Yet they always have the feeling that "people can tell". Between sessions, they wonder if they've got the lipstick off properly, or if they've remembered to put everything away. While dressing, they imagine that people can see through curtains, through walls. They jump at every creak of the floorboards. Thus the release of cross dressing is replaced by the fear of discovery, the guilt and secrecy. They feel that social attitudes are such that they dare not speak of it to anyone. There is a feeling of loneliness in having to keep it to oneself. Such TV's often don't know, or don't believe, that there are others like them, they certainly don't discuss it with any one. They shy away from any mention of it in the media. They wouldn't be able to bring themselves to watch a television programme about the subject, especially if the family were present. They often begin to acquire wardrobes of their own, hidden away with great cunning. It is no accident that my first book was called "The Secret Wardrobe".

Rachel tells how she used to she used to keep her clothes sealed in a plastic bag, hidden in the water cistern. Amanda wrote an article in "Chit-Chat" called "Hiding Places I have Known", places such as the back of her toy cupboard, in an old stove in the back yard (until her father decided to burn some rubbish in it) and inside her hi-fi cabinets in place of the wadding.

The house that I lived in had hollow lath and plaster walls which made an ideal hiding place. At one time, I had to spend several weeks in Newcastle on a training course, so I hid a cache of clothes inside the cushion of the back seat of my car. One weekend, we took a family trip somewhere, during which, my eldest son complained bitterly about how uncomfortable he was. He was sitting on one of my high heels.

Over a long period "in the closet", the cross-dressing urge varies in intensity. But the secrecy and deception goes on, and the revulsion at what one is. At times, one feels completely masculine and revolts against the double life to such an extent that one vows never to cross-dress again. From time to time, like many another TV, I would dispose of my complete wardrobe on the bonfire. Many TV's burn hundreds of pounds-worth of clothing in a lifetime.

It is interesting that burning is the usual method for disposal, rather than other methods. The ashes, with their tell-tale hooks and eyes are scattered and dug into the ground, to eliminate the remote possibility that they could be traced back. Much of this book was written while I was staying at a friend's house. Every scrap of discarded paper was taken to work to put in the company skip, rather than worrying my friends with the risk incurred by putting anything in the dustbin.

There is something especially final in burning something. Think of book burning, and feminists burning their bra's. But the urge always comes back. In the end, I accepted that it would. I knew that I would start stealing my wife's clothes again, so I kept my secret wardrobe, but made it difficult to get at. I told myself I could always dress if I wanted to, but agreed with myself that it was too much trouble to retrieve it. Somehow one comes to realise that the urge will always be there. Cross-dressing is not a passing phase. It is often said that "Transvestism is for life" and I know a number of TV's that are in their eighties and nineties. Many are very spry and fit. Is it possible that they have found an effective, if un-orthodox, palliative for life's stresses?

Since it is done in secret, the TV can never dress when and where he wants to. So he takes what chances are offered, when his wife is out, or when he goes away on business. One of my friends joined the Air Force as an armourer, as he says, "to prove to myself that I was a Man", but he found himself booking into hotels for weekends to spend lonely stolen moments of dressing, something that many TV's do.

Opportunity is rarely at a time or a place when the transvestite feels the urge, and afterwards there is guilt, and fear of discovery. TV's often dream of being able to dress when and where they want to. They may dream of living permanently as a woman. Usually restricted to the bedroom, or the attic, or the garden shed or to periods away from home, they long to "extend the closet" to the rest of the house, or the outside world. The urge builds up into an obsession and they may develop an excessive, but furtive, interest, not only in underwear shops, but in the ladies' departments and windows of chain stores.

The sum of all the stresses in one's life, lack of money, insecurity at work, troubles at home and so on, can give rise to more serious problems. From the moment we are born, we "hold in" emotions. They may be small, like not being allowed to have a toy that one wants and yet being forbidden to express displeasure, through to attending a serious accident and having to work through the horror. There are many good reasons why we should hold onto some emotions, for a while, at least. The mind's defences enable us to forget those we hold on to, but they can build up as stress. We may feel tense. The heart and the breathing may remain in a state of readiness for a reaction that never comes. At the worst they can exacerbate psychoses or reduce our resistance to infection, at the least they can result in tension, with muscular reactions leading to aches and pains and cramps. For some people, they can surface unexpectedly. They can't remember why, but they experience some of the physical symptoms of fear, in panic attacks, often with what is known as hyper-ventilation. One might "gobble" one's food without attending to one's eating, maybe swallowing excess air, causing digestive troubles. This shouldn't stop anyone from going to see a doctor, but if he can find nothing wrong then, perhaps, one should look within oneself. To deny one's feelings and emotions is to add to the stress. To acknowledge them allows a logical approach to them. There is a paradox in that, often, someone is so full of stress, that the act of will in going to see a counsellor takes him past the limit of what he can bear, so he never goes.

Some, TV's, in trying to escape from their feelings, may become introspective and remote. They may, in their pre-occupation, become less communicative. It takes up a part of their attention and they may throw themselves into practical matters such as work, or jobs around the house, yet not seem to achieve very much. If they are prone to bouts of depression, these may be deeper or longer lasting.

Alternatively, some people may subconsciously counter feelings of "not being a man" by becoming excessively so, especially if the social group in which they have grown up, or in which they live or work, is particularly repressive. In trying to forget about it, or to prove their masculinity, they may start drinking too heavily, or indulging in excessively macho activities, like driving too fast and aggressively. One might wonder whether such people can solve a drink problem, without first solving their cross-dressing problem.

In either case, what the family may see is a husband who is increasingly moody and erratic, with periods of more relaxed behaviour. Sometimes, he may react by having spells of being unbearably macho and hard on the children. Eventually, it may reach a crisis, which, if it takes place very quickly, may be particularly distressing to him and to those around him.

He may never tell anyone about being a transvestite, but blame it on other things. If he is already taking drugs, either illicit, or prescribed, he may just decide to end it all. There may be a major urge to break out, either to disclose or to run away and disappear. He may reject the male life altogether. A heavy drinker may become an alcoholic. Or he may lash out, verbally or physically. Often it will be his wife and family, sometimes it will be an unfortunate helpline worker.

The majority of TV's report that there has been some period when they wished with all their hearts that they could be women. They may even have become jealous of their wife's, or for that matter, any woman's femininity. They find themselves looking at a woman and imagining themselves like her and, at the same time, their male side is looking at her as a man would. At any given moment, depending which side is driving them, they may swing one way or the other. When I was younger, like any man, I would visualise myself, say, holding a girl in my arms on a crowded dance floor, soft and warm and yielding. (I never imagined myself being held by a man, as it were, dancing backwards). Yet another day, I would see a girl and imagine myself being her, living her life. I can't describe the exact feelings I had. In the closet, undeclared, there can, for some TV's, come a time when these feelings meet each other head on. No wonder they speak of confusion, when they ring the helpline.

All our lives, we all, consciously or unconsciously, take to ourselves many different role models at different times. It is how we learn. We look at others and copy those parts of them that we feel to be good. For some people, the models presented to them by their own sex may not provide all the attributes that "fit" their individual personality.

The TV associates with various male role models mostly, but female ones sometimes. What better one than someone he loves? It is not uncommon for a TV to say to his wife, "I love you so much, I want to be like you!". To the wife, this is often seems a particularly specious, not to say unbelievable, excuse. Yet it occurs to me that it might spring from a motivation that exists deep down in the TV's consciousness. There is a mechanism in which valued attributes of a person, especially a loved one, are taken in and experienced as our own, so that the TV may want to incorporate symbols of his wife's femininity into his own self. I remember there was a short term fashion for skirts with pleated hems. They looked so good on girls that I admired that I bought one. You could say that the slavishness with which we followed fashions up to the sixties was commercialised role modelling. Perhaps the sign of a mature Society is the lack of need to wear uniforms.

I have already suggested that the build-up of fantasy can lead the more erotic TV to various sexual exploits. The TV whose motives are gender based, may build up a very vivid picture of himself as a woman, sometimes with a disregard to his real body shape. He may get to the point where he really does see "a beautiful woman looking back at him from the mirror". If he is fighting against this other part himself, or has feelings that it is rejected by others, it may cause him, finally, to assert it. There is often a history of rejection of a part of him, somewhere in the past, either by the TV himself, or those around him. The TV may feel driven to do anything to find a resolution. He may not feel complete as a person, and may see the "sex change" as the only solution, throwing away all the male attributes in disgust, hoping that he will then be more complete, and progressing to full transexualism. I feel very strongly that this solution is encouraged by the media giving so much, usually favourable, publicity to men who have "changed sex", while refusing to acknowledge transvestites. Many men seek gender reassignment, as it were, straight from the closet. Possibly, if they spent some time among the transvestite community, talking, listening and learning how to express their female self in a way that doesn't overcome their male side, some might feel able to cope without changing over fully.

The general message is that cross-dressing is recreation, like any other hobby, an opportunity to express another side of oneself, so long as it does not cause harm or hurt to one's self or another. The transvestite acknowledges this need to conform to role models that are not seen to be masculine, but can build two separate persona in one person. On the one hand, the obsession, in the closet particularly, can cause a TV to forget the value of his male life. On the other, the exploration of this other side of himself can make his male side more secure. He finds a way to be a man sometimes and a woman sometimes.

Chapter 10
TRANSEXUALS

If you take the broad view, a transvestite could be anyone who wears the clothing of the opposite sex, for whatever reason. It could then be said that a transexual is then someone who crosses the sexual or gender boundaries, even if only for a short period. While most transexuals want to be women, some simply don't want to be men. It may be all in the mind, but it is none the less real for all that. So real that transexuals have been known to resort to self mutilation. One is on record as having taken a shotgun to his genitalia. There are also transexuals who are not comfortable with either gender role and live in a sort of limbo, or they may simply feel unable to project a dual gender image, as a transvestite does.

A consultant makes little distinction, but deals with the person as he is. The actual definition is not that easy to make. After all, it is not usually capable of a clear diagnosis, like a medical or physical condition. It is not the same as hermaphroditism, where the person appears to have physical characteristics of both sexes and may have been wrongly categorised at birth. Even if there is some hormonal imbalance, either spontaneous, or as the result of an accident, a man or woman may not necessarily see himself or herself as transexual, and the idea that some are "chromosomal transexuals" is, at the date of writing this, still unproven.

When I was in my teens, there was a small item in the Daily Telegraph about an ex-racing car driver, who had undergone a operation to change sex. I think it must have been Roberta Cowell, but the description given made it seem that there were some kind of physiological reasons. Whether this was true, or not, although there were a series of such re-assignments, from as long ago as the early thirties, on various people, very little was said about them. There were short reports in the news, from time to time, often sensationalised, or trivialising, but they were always something that happened to someone else.

Over the last twenty years, more and more people have talked about themselves, both TV's and TS's. Newspaper reports have become more detailed (and sensationalised), and a number of TS's have published autobiographies. In addition, there has been a general examination of gender roles, in popular songs, and by the artistes, with the emergence of gay society, and the development of the Women's movements. "Gender Bending" has become more and more exploited by the sex industry, in magazines featuring she-men, usually extremely glamorous, and other cross-gender scenarios, as well as stories of men being feminised by hormones, and becoming "the woman they always wanted to be".

The unfortunate part of it all is that people think that, by some wonderful pill, or the magic of the surgeon's knife, they can instantly be transformed. In public, the term tends to be reserved for those who actually have made the decision to change over; in other words, those who find life as a man totally intolerable. The chances of anyone being a genuine transexual are slim; for every TS, there are at least two hundred transvestites.

The hard truth is that people who are truly transexual are very rare and the sex change, properly called "gender reassignment", takes many years of sheer hard work, pain and even danger. The operation is not a change of sex, it is a change of role, with some surgical and chemical reconstruction. The important thing to keep in mind is that anyone can change their body, no-one can change themselves.

There are some people whose life experience was such that they had no other choice. Whatever their appearance in those interminable "before and after" pictures, the one feature they share is a strong and stable personality and a positive approach to life. You don't get to be an international model, just by having a pretty face.

What we have to consider is, how desperate we need to be before we go to the lengths of having our bodies changed, and whether we need let it alter our lifestyle. In other words, even if we are transexual, do we also have to be women? Anyone contemplating "changing over" has some hard questions to answer. Does he see himself as he really is, or does he still see himself in the image of his imagination? Even TV's who have been out of the closet for years find it difficult to shake off the feelings of guilt, the knowledge of what people might think of them. It is a compelling dream to wave a piece of paper and say, "Look, I'm a real woman! My surgeon says so!"

But, from the teenager who always felt uncomfortable with the role assigned to him, to the mature adult who has achieved an outwardly successful lifestyle, even helping to bring up a family, there are people that come to a point where they cannot continue to progress, or even survive as men. The issue is not as straightforward as is generally portrayed, and there a range of options that can be taken up.

Helplines are used to callers asking where they can obtain hormones, the object in the caller's mind being a longing for "real" breasts. I would not dismiss these people as "mere fetishists", but it is possible that they have let their preoccupation with their fantasy self run away with them. They haven't stopped to consider how they're going to hide them when they go out as a man, nor what the reaction would be from a prospective lady friend. With the stress of being in the closet, the gender urge can become an obsession. I have talked about the sexual fantasy merging into reality. In the same way, the gender aspect builds up as a fantasy.

There is the suggestion that one aspect of transvestism and, especially, transexualism, is the avoidance of the taboo of homosexuality. The idea is that, by changing role, people can meet their attraction to the originally opposite sex, yet remain heterosexual. It is true that some, who ask for the operation, do so because they cannot accept their homosexuality and there are some who admit their homosexuality and simply want to find a "straight" partner. There are men who have obtained breasts, while keeping their male genitalia, either to give satisfaction as both a man and a woman, or because they see themselves as the feminine half of a couple. In this, they consider the method of loving to be immaterial to the love itself, bearing in mind that, after the operation, a transexual cannot conceive. However, practically all gay men are happy to be so, they like their maleness and have no wish to change their bodies.

Although many transexuals have said that at one time they thought they must be gay, because they were attracted to men, they found that they needed to be seen as a woman, and to be treated as one. They wished to love a man as a woman would, and be loved by him as a woman. There are, in fact, many male to female transexuals who were always committed heterosexuals, as man to woman, and were only sexually attracted to women. They have married and brought up families. Approximately twenty per cent of transexuals, even though they adopt a totally female lifestyle, continue to be sexually attracted to women. The need of these so-called Lesbian Transexuals, is to adopt the female life pattern as completely as possible, and sexual considerations are secondary. It can be seen that even transexuality is not a straightforward issue.

There are others, for whom the name Trans-homosexual has been coined, who are nominally heterosexual, but are attracted to homosexual persons of the opposite sex, if you can see what I mean. They see themselves as being of the opposite gender, but homosexual. Such people do not always cross dress and usually have no reservations about their body, or their role in life in their biological gender. The visualisation is of, for instance, a woman who is assertive and happier in the company of men who are not overbearing. She would not see herself as a lesbian, being sexually attracted to men, but would prefer homosexual men and identify herself as one. Similarly one could visualise a man, who functions perfectly well in daily life, but is not assertive in his approach to women, or in sexual encounters. It is all to do with the complicated interaction between one's "self model" and one's "relationship model".

As with transvestites, there seem to be fewer female to male transexuals. Perhaps this is because women seem more casual about labels than men. The boundary between lesbians and female-to-male transexuals seems less clearly defined. Unity Hall, who came into prominence in the mid-thirties, is called a lesbian in some books, a transexual in others. It seems much easier for a transexual woman to find peace in the lesbian community, than it is for a man to do so in the gay male one. Nevertheless, the figure for women seeking gender re-assignment has recently started to rise quite rapidly.

There are transexuals who "came through the ranks" as transvestites. Occasionally, a TV, still living a fantasy, will carry it so far that he has a sexual relationship with a man, and is badly injured, emotionally, by the experience, when he wakes up in the morning and he is himself again. It is easy to suggest that one should prepare oneself emotionally for what one is about to do, less easy to do so in practice.

But others, as they become more level-headed, are able to learn about themselves and others and, seeing themselves clearly, can discover their true feelings. The vast majority of transvestites simply dress in a totally social scenario. Others may have transexual leanings, and be able to explore calmly and may decide to cope without changing over, or be able to approach the concept in a reasoned manner.

There are those who have a deep rooted desire to be female, and have an absolute conviction of their inner femininity, yet have never felt the need to cross-dress. There are some that simply want to get rid of their male organs and don't really mind whether they appear male or female. There are some that deal with it in a cerebral manner (I think the person who said that was having a sly dig at me!).

For some, the only reason for changing over is that they are completely at odds with being a man, and the urging of their maleness is a constant reminder that they are what they don't want to be. A very small minority simply loath men. As one said "I hate men. They're arrogant, messy, smelly fools." Or another, "Men are all the same. All they think of is sex and telling dirty stories". Perhaps they may be rejecting the maleness that they still feel in themselves.

To many transexuals, sexual considerations are secondary to the need to acquire a body which accords with their feelings about themselves. Anyone contemplating the "sex change" should look at himself carefully. Someone may be unsuccessful as a man but, if he is unsuccessful as a person, he is unlikely to succeed by simply changing his bodyshape. In the absorption with dressing and the concept of womanhood, he may have neglected his male life. If he has let himself go, in his home life and his job, this may have produced new problems. He may have let his TVism take over his life, to the exclusion of other activities.

There are many people living in their chosen lifestyle permanently, without bothering to have an operation and, incidentally, without worrying that they are then classed as transvestites.

If the prospective TS finds the male role totally unsupportable, and needs to take on the female role, does he need to take on the female biological role as well, in particular the female sexual role? On the other hand, if he feels that he can only make love as a woman, and needs the operation, does it need to affect his everyday lifestyle?

Many transexuals, even in their male guise, are visibly feminine, either in their appearance or their behaviour. Liz Hodgkinson, in her book 'Bodyshock' gave a fair and sympathetic view of such transexuals. I feel that she failed to bring out the basic characteristic, the essential femininity of many of them. This may, possibly, be because she, naturally, takes her own femininity for granted. Moreover, most of the outwardly successful changed over TS's were always very feminine in their looks; their features never began to take on that typically masculine look as they grew into their teens.

It is undeniable that the potential transexual who wishes to pass as a woman, must have that total conviction of his femaleness, to be able to carry it off, day in and day out, for life. However, a good gender identity counsellor or consultant doesn't reject someone because he doesn't look like a woman, or because he has a voice like drill sergeant. He might have a deep voice, a heavy growth of facial hair, prominent Adam's Apple, receding hairline and other characteristically masculine features, and it is most unlikely that he could ever pass in public as a woman, despite the best will in the world. Often the urge is so strong that he may have great difficulty in accepting the facts, and some people put great pressure on consultants to help them "change sex".

Consultants see their duty as being to protect someone from setting out on a potentially disastrous course of action, but I have met transexuals who appear to have been attended to by people who presumably had some arbitrary model of what constitutes a transexual. They had been simply rejected and dropped back into the water, to sink or swim, even though they may have been in greater emotional distress than any obviously transexual client and needed all the more support.

Chapter 11
CHANGING OVER

Since the object of 'changing over' is to live as a woman, it seems reasonable to suggest the prospective TS should try it. In fact, helplines are increasingly receiving phone calls from people who say that they want to change sex, yet seem to have little idea of what is involved. In some cases, they have not even talked about it to their wives and families.

In fact, living as a woman is one of the first things the consultant will suggest. The whole emphasis of this book is that the need to change over is a stress, partly sexual, and made more intense by lack of opportunity to express one's femininity. Thus the therapy is to reduce the stress by giving the TV "permission" to dress as often as possible, to dispel the guilt and increase the opportunity.

It is also one of the requirements to be considered for surgery, that the potential TS has lived as a woman completely, for a number of years, and is supporting him (or her) self, before surgery, or even medication, can go ahead. This is the so-called 'life test', and no reputable consultant will proceed without it.

So it follows that it might be no bad idea for anyone who thinks that he is transexual to 'come out' fully as a TV for a period first, to talk to others, to absorb their ideas and pick up the information necessary to decide whether he really needs to go all the way, to live as a 'constructed woman', not just from time to time, but every day and every hour for the rest of his life. Sooner or later, the potential TS is going to have to be a full time woman. He needs to get his act together. Joining a local transvestite group will let him practice in safety. He can also talk to people and compare their experiences with his own. Suddenly he is no longer on his own. One of the problems that all transvestites and transexuals face is that they feel 'different' from everyone else, so-called normal society. The stark fact is that they will always be different, but being part of a group may help them feel less different.

There may be other pre-op TS's there, full of their own plans, so he should keep his own counsel. I detect a very male tendency among some of them - the inability to change one's mind, or admit that one may be wrong. They may be so full of excitement, in their hopes for the future, that they can, unknowingly, exert a considerable peer pressure.

A useful first idea is to put all one's feelings down in a long letter, or to keep a secret diary, then send it to a specialist consultant or counsellor. The Beaumont Trust can arrange this. One thing that the prospective TS won't find in this book is pat answers. It is important that the TS should ask himself some searching questions and guard against realigning perceptions of past life to fit new feelings. Most people rewrite their life histories to conform with their present needs; what is needed is to extract those feelings which they may think are imposed, extract those that are wishful thinking, and then see what are left.

Whatever one has in one's mind, it can be helpful to talk to a counsellor, or a consultant, but one must be scrupulously honest. Many psychiatrists feel very strongly that some of their clients have memorised a string of cliches, heard in the transexual community, and are telling them what they think they want to hear. The only person a prospective TS can cheat is himself; it is all too easy to make a terrible mistake in changing over. Many TS's are so pre-occupied with conforming to some sort of transexual stereotype, that they blind themselves to the real issues in their lives, which surface after all the fuss of "the operation" is over.

Many TV's and TS's have had a rough time in childhood. Whether it was because of what they are, or they are what they are because of it, there is likely to be the results of the stresses, especially when you consider that there will be a hidden side that has been concealed for years. So, for the consultant, the possibity that his client is transexual is not the first concern. His, or her, first interest is a stable, positive approach to life, and a workable plan for the future, as counsellors say, "Well and truly in the here and now". There is a responsibility for the future quality of life. He will look at his client as a person, looking for problems that may not even be gender related, seeing it as his, or her, duty to encourage the client to sort them out first.

Every reputable consultant works to a document called "The Standards of Care for hormonal and surgical re-assignment of gender dysphoric persons", first laid out at a conference in the USA in 1979, and produced by the Harry Benjamin International Gender Dysphoria Foundation in America. The actual document runs to some twelve pages, copies may be obtained from the Beaumont Trust. Some of the main conclusions are that the patient should ideally be single in civil law and over 18 (sometimes over 21). Hormones should only be administered if it is safe medically. The patient should ideally present in a reasonably convincing manner, but more importantly, be able to form satisfactory crucial interactions with others and be accepted by others, whatever the role of adoption. Before being put on the waiting list for surgery, the patient must be living, working and functioning socially in the role of adoption.

Someone who sets out to be a Gender Identity Consultant will never be in an easy position. In the end, he has to rely on a subjective assessment based, not only his psychiatric training, but also on his experience of other clients. Doctors and psychologists work in gender identity clinics because they clearly recognise the difficulties and predicaments of transexual people. Whether "change" is possible or not, the staff set out to try to understand and support the person and, if considered helpful, to explain matters and counsel not only the individual but also family and friends and anyone else who might be able to help if they had a better understanding of the problem.

Usually, hormones are prescribed, the popular idea being that they will alter the body shape, producing the semblance of breasts and rounded hips. The physical changes which occur are, in fact, exaggerated by the popular press and further magnified by wishful thinking. There are no pills or potions that will produce a beautiful woman, or someone would be making a fortune!

The physical effects vary from one person to another. Everyone who sets out to "change over" thinks that he will be the exception, but it would seem likely that those "post-op" transexuals with a well rounded bust, are using surgical implants.

Prescriptions are never for more than three month's supply, and they are accompanied by careful interviews, in which the client reports his experience of the therapy. There are some who demand medication as a right, and get short shrift from the consultant and there are many that are less than honest about themselves. The actual reasons for prescribing hormones, and the effects they produce, are far more complex, but one effect is the reduction of the sexual urge, thus another source of stress is reduced. The wife should be made aware that what little sex life she had will disappear altogether. The effects are usually, but not always completely, reversed when medication stops. They don't reduce the attractiveness of women (or men); I suppose one is responding to learned sexual signals.

They have an effect on mood swings, though emotional effects may also be due to the TS "letting go". It has been reported that the TS becomes calmer, and any anti-social behaviour is reduced. I think that this may be so if it has occurred directly because of the transexual stress and frustration, but not if the person is basically amoral. Thus the TS may have been drinking heavily, with periods of violence or erratic behaviour.

Hormones are not prescribed lightly. It cannot be emphasised too highly that, in the required dosage, they are potentially life-threatening. It may be that the TS has some physical condition that would make them too dangerous. The possible harmful side effects have to be spelled out clearly, and the client's GP must be closely involved. The client's previous medical history must be considered, and, if hormones are taken in combination with some other forms of medication, serious side effects can occur.

The most serious effect is the increased tendency for the blood to clot. Blood clots can form anywhere, but there is a very real danger of "Deep Vein Thrombosis" in the legs, reducing the circulation and increasing the risk of gangrene in the case of injury. Sometimes such a clot breaks loose and can become lodged elsewhere in the body. The result can be that they lodge in the blood vessels of the lungs, (pulmonary embolism). In addition, fluid retention is increased, increasing the risk of hypertension (high blood pressure). Damage to the liver can produce jaundice, in fact, all the major organs of the body, including the heart, kidneys, brain and liver, are put under tremendous pressure, depending on the dose.

Hormones do not halt the growth of body hair, such as the beard. Nor do they repair the results of male pattern baldness, so the TS may for ever have to wear a wig, something that often becomes unbearably hot. The usual method for removing beard growth is electrolysis. This is a process whereby a fine needle is passed down the hair stem into the follicle, which is then cauterised by an electric current. Each hair has to be treated, one by one, and the current has to be judged accurately. It is not a pleasant experience, and the hair usually regrows two or three times. Only a small area can be treated at each session, the process may take two or three years for facial hair alone.

Hormone therapy cannot alter the bone structure in any way. One still has wide shoulders and narrow hips, a heavy forebrow and chin and, probably, a big nose. Though fat deposits are laid down on the hips and breasts primarily, they also tend to be distributed over the whole body. In combination with fluid retention, there is usually a gain in weight.

There is also no effect on the voice. To some extent the male voice develops physically during puberty; a man's voice tends to be deep, while a woman's tends to be higher, although a great deal of learning is involved. As his voice breaks, a boy is under social pressure to use the lower registers, to use the resonance of his throat. Part of the work in speech therapy is in avoiding this resonance, particularly when speaking more loudly. A transexual spends hour after hour learning to control the pitch and timbre of her voice, not only in conversation, but when talking above the background noise of, say, a party or a disco.

I have spoken with transexuals who have undergone an operation to alter their voices. Very few surgeons will undertake the work, for there is a good chance that something will go drastically wrong. Some of them sounded to me like people impersonating very camp men, for they had missed the point that women pace their speech in a different way to men, they place the emphasis on different words. But there are many women who have husky voices and the TS may be accepted if she has already been accepted on the basis of appearance.

Confusion will tend to arise on the telephone, especially if it is followed by a face to face meeting. Generally however, the main study must be the way women speak, their phrasing and mannerisms, and the way they approach others.

There must follow a long period of assessment and counselling before there is any thought of surgical intervention. The actual reassignment operation, is a major one, with possible complications. "Changing over" does not happen overnight. It takes many years of pain, both physical and emotional, and sheer hard work. The operation is not easily obtained through the National Health Service, there being a waiting list of several years. Most transexuals opt for private treatment, not only to reduce the delay, but because many feel that they should not divert scarce public funds. Nevertheless, they insist that NHS facilities should be available for those who need them. From beginning to end, and without any cosmetic surgery, the transexual will be lucky if he (or she) has spent less than £10,000 on the total process of changing over.

The operation lasts about four hours and, as may be expected with such radical surgery, is attended by a great deal of discomfort, and a long recuperation period. A graphic account is given in Liz Hodgkinson's "Bodyshock". It must also be remembered that surgeons are naturally very averse to interfering with an organic mechanism that is in working order. Because of the high risk that the transexual finds that the grass, in fact, is not greener on the other side, they insist on the client signing an indemnity.

It is becoming a cause of concern that hormones are becoming available through the black market. Someone who is desperate to achieve their aims will take anything, regardless of possible side effects. We already have the example of athletes who take anabolic steroids. I am told that ski-jumpers used to take arsenic. Hormones are just as dangerous and those who take them are taking a deliberate risk with their lives.

What can happen is that the transvestite, finding that the expected changes in his body don't happen as quickly as he expects, will increase the dose until he finishes up in hospital. Several such people can count themselves lucky to be alive, and some were not so lucky.

Chapter 12
AFTER THE CHANGE

Sooner or later, the TS will have to "come out", not just to the TV community, but to Society at large. To move from being a part time TV to living full time takes a great deal of planning. No-one can expect to live as a man, then walk out of the front door, one morning, and go to work, as a woman, however much they may fantasise that they can. To simply expect instant acceptance from everyone is courting disaster. The probable reaction will be derision from colleagues, even physical abuse, the sack, scandal among the neighbours and shame for his wife and family. One family reported that their children were bringing death threats home from school.

It is true that some TS's are changing over, very discreetly, in their present homes and workplaces. Usually there are special factors in their favour. Most transexuals, however, wish to live completely as a woman, with no one aware of any difference. This, almost always, means moving to a new location, leaving everything behind, and starting completely anew. It will be starting completely from scratch. If the TS is not at peace with herself, she is likely to find the loneliness and isolation a serious problem. With no references and no past history, she will not be able to get a job as good as the one she has left. Unskilled jobs for women are notorious for their poor pay and bad conditions. She will have to survive on a vastly reduced income, with higher expenses, cosmetics, hair care and, probably, continuing medical treatment. Without a past life, it will be difficult to get references for credit or insurance. Even though most documents can be changed to the new name, the past will keep coming back to haunt her.

Somehow, she has to learn all the subtle ways a woman speaks and acts, something women have had a lifetime to learn, and she has to unlearn all the little mannerisms that became habit as a man. Any TV will tell you how easy it is to be "read". The task of maintaining the image all day, every day, is immense. The TS may move from one location to another, over the years, as she becomes more integrated. This is the "real life" test. Each step is carefully planned, as the old life is dismantled, and the new one built up. Then, when she can demonstrate a settled existence, with a reasonable quality of life, the operation will be considered.

It is in coping with these day to day problems that the sharing of experiences by other TS's can be of help, along with the companionship. I have deliberately painted a black picture, but it is one that the prospective TS must be prepared for. There will be moments of despair, but there will also be moments of humour, if she will keep her mind open to them.

What is it all about? To describe one's feelings one has to relate them to more easily understood ones. We describe emotions by giving them names, and we assume that everyone feels them in the same way. If I tell people that I feel sad, they know what I mean, because they themselves have at some time also felt sad. How can I describe the feeling of being a transvestite?

It is suggested by some authorities that the difference between a TS, and a TV, is that the latter is quite clear about his male gender identity, but nevertheless likes to cross dress. How does one determine the clarity of a client's view of himself, bearing in mind that most TS's have learnt the right things to say? On the surface, to say that one is confused about one's gender identity is to suggest that one is not sure whether one is a man or a woman. The real meaning is much more subtle. One can be sure of one's identity, but not sure how it relates to a dualised society. One may have even been hiding from it for years, pushing it to the back of one's mind.

Do transexuals in childhood really think of themselves as being of the wrong sex, or do they simply dislike the sex they have been given?

In this Society, you have to align yourself with one faction or the other. If you can't relate to the male camp, you have to join the female camp. The more you try to force yourself into the wrong camp, the more the stress. The more defined the rules are for joining one camp or the other, the more difficult it will be to conform to them, but it saves a lot of pain, trouble and money, even danger, if you can visit the other from time to time on a temporary basis.

Having said all that, one asks, is there a point at which someone cannot exist, even as a transvestite and has to become a transexual? A point between thinking one is feminine and knowing it. There is a man to woman relationship that goes back into the ages. It is the basis of the family and the home. In passing, I feel very strongly that those extreme feminists that would reject it as they seek equality are in danger of throwing the baby out with the bath water. Somehow there are masculine and feminine differences that sprang up all those centuries back in Dr. Desmond Morris's jungle. Is there a boundary between these and the visualisations of gender role behaviour that we have built up since. Is it that transvestites can live with this deeper difference, but transexuals cannot?

If the TV has joined in a reasonably successful marriage, and produced children, it is likely that he has been enough of a man not to have been a "born" woman. He needs to ask himself how long has he really felt that he was female? Is it just that the grass seems greener on the other side of the fence? Is it just that he has found life as a man boring? The everyday world of a woman is just as likely to be so. He will almost certainly be finding that it is nice to put on the unfamiliar clothes, whenever he dresses, particularly swapping trousers for a skirt, and to see himself in an unfamiliar perspective. To face the world as a woman will be a new sensation, but within a few weeks it will be little different to living life as a man, except that a woman has, all the time, to put up with being patronised by men, and worse; it isn't all a matter of having doors opened for her. The TV should set out to find out what women's lives are really like. One freedom he will certainly miss is that of venting his feelings against, for instance, other road users. Can he restrain himself from the customary male salute to the driver who has just nearly run him over on a zebra crossing? Can he be compliant in the face of downright rudeness, without complaint or retaliation? Just how does he relate to other people; not only sexually, but in a man-man and man-woman interaction?

The Dual Role Transvestite solves the problem by building two persona which complement each other as expressions of his real self. Thus it is, that a very masculine man can speak of "the girl within", and the acknowledgement of this inner person, can help him stabilise and reinforce his masculine part. If he is, in his approach to others, a man, his sexuality is restricted to his male half. Even though he may experiment with female-type interactions, since he can hardly behave towards other people as a man when he is wearing a dress, he does not usually take them into a close, intimate or sexual relationship. This may be why a TV can say that his female role is non-sexual. Indeed, in his "female mode", he may see himself as sexless.

One could define three needs that a transexual may have: To be accepted by Society for what one is, whatever it is, to be accepted by a man as a woman and to be accepted by women as a woman.

As a transexual, the TV is likely to have to face considerable bigotry and prejudice, with no way of avoiding it, and, having rejected the male half of Society, is likely to find it very difficult to become accepted by the female half.

As regards acceptance by a man, I mean, acceptance as a partner. Quite often transexuals go right off the rails after their operation, trying out their new body and lifestyle. In casual relationships, their partners may detect nothing unusual. These TS's realise, like many a woman before them, how much these affaires are worth. One transexual, who was known to be such, soon realised that her success was nothing more than her novelty value. When it comes to a long term relationship, there is a problem. If the transexual does not disclose the true state of affairs, she is living a lie. On the other hand, by disclosing, she is taking the chance of losing her partner. Marriage is out of the question, since it is against the law.

Which then brings up the question of acceptance by Society. A transexual is still, in law, a man. Her birth certificate cannot be altered. Further, since the law sees her as a man, and does not recognise a man with a vagina, she cannot be raped. There is one way, of course, in which a man (or a woman) may be the unwilling victim of sexual intercourse. It is against the law, but is regarded as little more than common assault.

The inequalities and injustice of British law in regard to men and women, gay or straight, is a constant matter for discussion nowadays, but this is one aspect in which it demonstrates its archaic bigotry to the full. As I see it, any sexual violation is rape and it is time we moved into the twentieth century, especially since it is now nearly the twenty first.

It will also be necessary to give thought to a mutually supportive end to the marriage. There has, in any case, to be a divorce. Although there are stories of the two people living together as friends, it doesn't often work out. In a way the TS is trying to have his cake and eat it. The TS's former wife has a right to find another man, and a right to a sex life. Meanwhile, the TS may well be looking for a man friend of her own. Thus there is a tendency for them to be rivals. But, in any case, both have new lives to start, and they need to forget the old.

Apart from the birth certificate, most papers, such as driving licences, bank accounts, social security and tax records can be altered to reflect the new identity. If it is necessary to produce the birth certificate on seeking employment, for instance to enrol in a company pension scheme, it can usually be done in confidence. There are transexuals in every city in the land who, after maybe twenty years hard work, are living and working as women, with few people being aware of their past.

Some gain a high profile in the press, often unwanted and unasked. Sooner or later someone will find out, as happened with Tula and Mark Rees, although it must be said that both of these people were adopting a high profile in any case. Others find their chosen vocation makes it necessary to disclose, or they simply feel that they must be honest.

While there are many transexuals who, after all the hard work, have achieved a satisfying lifestyle, this does not always happen and the belief that one could live in the adopted gender role remains a less than perfect success. Often there is sense of anti-climax. For, perhaps, ten years "changing over" has occupied almost all of the TS's attention. Suddenly, there may be an emptiness to life.

From the transvestite opting to stay in the closet to the fully changed over and apparently successful transexual, everyone has to find the compromise that will give them the most peace of mind. A transexual is said to be born different and she will be for ever different. At its best, gender reassignment is no more than a surgical reorganisation. No man can ever become a real woman, no woman a real man. Some transexuals ask for operation after operation, to fit breast implants, to reshape the features and the figure. Usually, the surgeon puts his foot down, for they will forever be chasing the end of the rainbow, almost cosmetic surgery fetishists. In the end, it is still one's own eyes looking back out of the mirror.

Could it be said that, to live completely as if one were a woman, is to live a lie just as surely as if one continued to live as a man?

There are some who simply accept the difference and enjoy themselves as human beings. Rachael Webb suggests that to openly admit to being transexual may invite prejudice, but to deny it is to negate all one's previous life, which may in many ways have been just as valuable. She says "I was a lorry driver before, and I take pride in that life, just as I take pride in my present life."

Why should we reject the good in our past lives, along with the bad, just because we are not what Society says we should be? I was father to a family once, and that is something more precious than anything. I don't make any great secret of being transexual or transvestite, or whatever, but I don't rub peoples noses in it. I value the friends I have, and that friendship comes about because I am me, and I am what I am because of the things that have gone past. I have no regrets, nor do I see any reason to complain. The past is to learn from, to make the present build a positive future.

Chapter 13
COMING OUT

Sooner or later, most TV's "come out" of the closet. It may be by confession, they may be discovered or their wives may set out to confront them.

The first contact most TV's make with the world outside is to phone a helpline. However much of a comfort the Samaritans may be, most TV's like to talk to someone who has gone through the same problems. In many cities, they can recommend a local transvestite phone number, and they will have taken good care to assure themselves of its credibility. Most gay helplines, such as FRIEND, also offer this facility.

It takes a great deal of courage to make that first call. Not only is the TV telling someone else for the first time, but he is also, for the first time, admitting, to himself, what he is. Often at the last vital moment the TV cannot bring himself to speak. Each week the log book records one "silent call" after another. A good helpline, although not usually advertising itself as being a counselling service, should set out to work to a clear code of ethics and practice. I would like to see them follow the example of other helplines, such as FRIEND, the gay helpline, who are members of the British Association for Counselling. The main feature of their ethic is that the call is strictly confidential. Another is "respect for the dignity and worth of every human being".

But however much support the helpline gives, my feeling is that it is a form of first aid. The immediate problem is alleviated, but there has been no long term solution and no plan for the future. That is the real purpose of this book and others like it. I have tried to be as honest as I can be. In fact, I may have upset some of my fellow TV's and TS's.

The TV may, in fact, not wish to go any further, and the helpline is always there, but discovering that he is, after all, not alone, then the TV may wish to hear from others and compare his experiences with theirs. Every TV has to follow his own path, but the only way to learn is to talk and listen and observe. One way is to join one of the national groups that publish regular journals. These contain articles which recount the feelings and experiences of other TV's. Often the articles are helpful in the relationship with a wife and family. For the TV on his own, the magazines are a lifeline to the outside world. In addition, there are meetings in most major cities of the country.

Coming out is not an instantaneous process. It takes months or years. I would like to think that, for my readers, it is a learning and growing process. I have already written about the sense of relief at the end of the secrecy, yet some TV's also have to cope with a sense of loss. In the past, whenever they had a session of dressing, whatever their other feelings, there would be the edge of excitement from the idea of doing something forbidden, the surge from the fear of discovery. In fact, having got so used to suffering secrecy and guilt, some may find that there is a very real gap in their lives. Human nature is contrary!

To meet your first TV is a daunting prospect. Whatever you've been told or read, it still comes as a shock to find that he really is just like any other bloke. The meeting will be in some public area, such as a well-lit, busy shopping mall, a cafe or a pub. Unless the befriender is a transexual, both will usually be dressed as men. It is often difficult to talk about one's transvestism right away. The conversation may, initially, be about trains or football, for it is a standing joke among TV's that so many members are railway or tramcar nuts. Often the other TV will start the ball rolling by talking, quietly, of his background, and the realisation comes that he's just the same, and has gone through all the same internal struggles.

When the TV goes courting, and finds the girl who is to be his wife, the idea of cross-dressing may be forgotten altogether. He has never spoken of it, but he won't have told anyone. In between sessions he won't have even admitted it to himself. It is not uncommon for a TV to be confronted with the evidence and still deny it. In teenage, particularly, he swings between being all man and 'not man'. It is not simply that he thinks he will be 'cured' by marriage. Especially when he is courting, he is all man. Even if he allows himself to think about it, the urge is gone and he does not expect it to come back. But, as the first flush of romance dies away, particularly with the ready access to female clothes, his wife's, the cross-dressing may return.

Many transvestites dress in complete secrecy for many years and, to their fear of the attitude of Society and friends and the possible shame of their sexuality, is added the knowledge of a long-held secret guilt in their marriages.

In many cases, transvestite's wives are thrown into it by accidental discovery. In an ideal world, all TV's would confess, preferably before they married, but, perhaps I have, to an extent, explained why, all too often, they don't. Perhaps if future years can dispel some of the ignorance, guilt and shame, this will happen.

While some of the books on transvestism are written by accepting wives or lovers, most are written by confirmed bachelors. It is easy for them to talk about communication or, as in my case, to be wise after the event. When you are married and living with someone, if often isn't easy to talk about some things, particularly when you're not clear about them yourself, and after all those years of silence. But once the talking starts it must be a two way thing. Somewhere a compromise has to be found and the more both partners can open their minds and hearts to each other the better.

Many successful transvestite marriages are second, or late, marriages, where the TV, through maturity or bitter experience, knows that it will not go away, and has confessed beforehand, but more and more young people are also telling the truth to their future wives, who in turn are trying to be supportive. It has to be said that, even given the prior choice of whether to go through with it, few wives say they had any real idea of what they were letting themselves in for. Unlike a medical condition, or a disability, there is nothing to see. It is an intangible that even their husbands barely comprehend.

There are some wives who have sensed that something was wrong. They wondered why their husband was so irritable and remote, somehow always pre-occupied. They often came to the conclusion that they had found another woman. In some cases, the husband's distress was so apparent, that his wife urged him to tell her what, on earth, was the matter. Often the news came almost as an anticlimax; many wives have said that their first reaction was "Oh! Is that all!"

Some wives don't seem to see the cross-dressing itself as a problem, but are more worried about the effect on their relationship, on family and friends, and they worry about the future. There is the fear of the unknown, what it is going to mean to the family and how far he will want to go.

If the TV's wife knows, or suspects, that her husband is cross-dressing, but won't admit it, several options may occur to her. She may drop hints that she knows about it, or leave helpful books lying around.

The possibility may occur to her of either trying to catch him in the act, or of confronting him with her knowledge or with evidence. If this is the plan, it will need great care and sensitivity. Many men in this position are carrying an unimaginable burden of guilt and shame, not only because of what they are, but from all the years of deception and secrecy. Though the TV, possibly, can't understand why, he may know somehow, that he is in the grip of an urge he can't control. If cornered in the process, the natural reaction could be panic. Being forced to confront himself in a violent way, could trigger a violent reaction. Even the most mild mannered man could lash out and cause real injury, or, not only to avoid facing facts, but to stop himself from violence, he may run away.

A helpline once received a call from a transvestite's wife, because her husband had disappeared and had been missing for three days. She found a telephone number, written on a scrap of paper, in his car, and telephoned to find out whose it was. Martine Rose tells the story of a TV leaving his wife in these circumstances. In her distress she did everything she could to find him, looking for, and visiting, groups all over the country. This story has a happy ending, for, in the end, he was reunited with his family. But I suspect, some families, especially in the past, have simply not bothered to look.

A secret is never easy to keep. As humans, we have a need to share. The motto of the Trans-Net helpline is "Talk to Someone". One of the most frequent questions asked of helplines is whether the TV should confess to his wife, and how to go about it. Those TV's that feel compelled to confess the truth, often go about it in entirely the wrong way. Unfortunately, there isn't a single right way, because every TV is different, and so is every wife. Helplines have to be very wary when a caller says that he wants to confess. Any comment by the operator is likely to be taken as tacit permission to go ahead, and some callers get quite upset when they are not given it. One thing the helpline operator will ask, if the caller admits that he is using his wife's clothes, is how he would like someone to wear his clothes without his permission.

Where he has been using his wife's underclothes, she has every right to consider that her most personal and private possessions have been violated. The emotions it produces may go even deeper. I have already talked about the feelings produced for many TV's of taking on the attributes of the original wearer. The TV's wife may feel this too, and feel that her person is being taken over in a very real way.

It would be would be nice to think that confession, when it finally comes about, does so out of guilt at the deceit. More often, I'm afraid to say, it may simply be to extend the closet, to end the isolation or to find company in his dressing. He may be trying to counter the guilt by looking for someone who will accept him as he is. If he can find any sort of approval, he can say "If she thinks it's alright, it must be".

One might expect someone who has had something on his mind for twenty or thirty years would be pre-occupied with it, but some TV's are unbelievably self-centred. This is a composite of some of the interviews we have undertaken, happily a minority. The first thing the transvestite said was, "I've just told my wife about it. What do I do now?" We pointed out that the TV had dropped a lifetime's worry on to his wife in thirty seconds flat and asked how she was. He replied "I don't know, I told her in the middle of a quarrel and she's gone to her mother's". And then he had the unbelievable gall to say "I don't know what she's bothering about. It's nothing to do with her!" This after years of marriage.

But we have other TV's, unashamedly crying, saying "How can I go on like this? I know this is something inside me that I can't stop, but I just can't tell anyone. I love my wife, I love my children and they love me. I couldn't bear to hurt them or to lose their love. How can I admit to them that I am not the man they think I am?"

It is a classic Catch 22 situation; tell and be damned, not tell and be damned. What can anyone say, except suggest that the caller phones the helpline whenever he wants to talk to someone and get things off his chest? Hopefully media coverage will help TV's to broach the subject gently. When the Sheffield Star printed a half page article about a transvestite and his wife, one man asked his wife "Cor! What do you think of them then?" As it happened, his wife simply said "Well, they enjoy it, and it does no harm." Luckily he had the sense to proceed cautiously in his disclosure. Over a number of days, he built up to his confession. In this case his wife finally agreed to see him dressed up, and went further in setting out to get him some decent clothes, and to sort out his amateurish attempts at make-up. But he was still lucky. It is one thing to accept the idiosyncrasies of others, quite another when someone close to you is involved.

Some TV's, as the need to disclose builds up along with their fear of doing so, finally do something drastic. At all costs they have to find a way of "breaking the ice". Sometimes a transvestite makes semi-accidental slips, like being careless about removing make-up, leaving items of clothing, cosmetics, or compromising books lying around. Thus the emotional distress and confusion for his wife is compounded. Probably, the worst possible way is for him to appear before her fully dressed. He, in his fantasy, thinks he looks absolutely stunning. What his wife sees is a child dressing up, but under all that makeup and the ill-fitting clothes, unaccountably is the shape of her husband, the man she thought she'd married.

If the TV has not sorted himself out first, disclosure may be the worst thing he can do. He may still be unsure of himself, on the defensive. He may not have worked out all the likely reactions to his disclosure, his as well as hers. There is the story of the TV who confessed and found his wife supportive, but then felt bitterly ashamed, because he felt himself to be less of a man for her. So the disclosure may bring new doubts:

"Does she see me as less of a man?", "Does she really understand, or is she only humouring me?", "Will she go off and find a 'real man'?". Understanding may take years of loving work together, by both husband and wife.

Another point that could be made about finding out first what it means to him, is that, if the TV decides to confess, he can explain it reasonably, without too much drama. If he is highly stressed and emotional, his wife will be bound to reflect his feelings and be much more worried than she might otherwise be.

Chapter 14
THE MARRIED TV

It must not be assumed that a TV's wife will invariably reject the idea out of hand, but many TV's expect to confess and find instant acceptance. While it something that he has been dealing with for many years, to his wife it is a whole new concept.

Her first reaction may well be shock and disbelief, not knowing know whether to laugh at the idea of her husband togged up in a dress, bulging in all the wrong places, or to cry at the enormity of the idea that this person who she once thought was her man, for all those years, was never the person she thought he was.

I hope to show that there is a positive way forward, unconventional though it may be. It isn't a stopgap to solve the husband's problems in the short term; it is a whole new way of marriage. There are many TV's wives who say that there is a sense of sharing, and as fulfilling a life together as any of the best marriages.

The transvestite's wife has her own identity and world view. She is not the meek little stereotype, accepting anything, so long as it is explained to her. It would be a reasonable reaction to say "I married a man, not a woman!" It is at such a time as this that one examines one's own self and one's motivations. Some women have a very fixed notion of the places in which wives and husbands fit into the family structure. The reaction to the idea that the husband is a transvestite is that their place in the scheme of things is being eroded. They may feel that, at all costs, they must preserve their place as wife and mother, and the stereotyped role of their men as husband and father. Indeed, some regard their husband as their property and cannot accept anything that they see as devaluing him. For some women, the idea grates against something deep inside. It may go so against the grain that a TV's wife simply cannot tolerate it. That is her privilege. She could, quite reasonably feel that she has been dropped into a situation that is none of her making, and feel that she wants none of it. In the end, the decision is hers. Particularly, if she has been kept in the dark for many years, she may feel that she has been sold a duff bill of goods.

For most wives, at first, there is the feeling that the even flow of life and the security of a stable domestic life is threatened. The husband may provide a sense of security. The idea that he is not as strong as she thought may cause a wife to feel that the very foundations of her marriage are shifting. She may have a feeling of helplessness or a feeling of guilt, and feel that she has failed, somehow, as a woman. She may ask herself where she went wrong, or what she could have done differently. In this, she has something in common with many other wives, even where things, on the surface, seem innocent. For instance, wives who are looking after their invalid husbands often experience tremendous guilt feelings, wishing they could do more, wishing they'd stopped him smoking or eating too many chips. The fact is, that it is something that has been with her husband for years.

Probably, the most serious effect is the feeling of a breach of trust. Inevitably, a wife will wonder what else there is she does not know. The answer is that, if he says there is nothing, he is probably telling the truth. The likelihood of there being other secrets is no more than in any other marriage.

Many wives reject their husband's transvestism completely. They simply don't want to consider any alternative to a husband who behaves "as a man". The husband is forced to stay in the closet, becoming more and more frustrated, probably more and more erratic and bad-tempered, or more and more withdrawn. In these circumstances, it is unlikely that the marriage will continue for very long, even if his wife is heavily dependent on him for the upkeep of the home and provision for the family.

In many marriages it is kept a hidden thing. The husband is "allowed" to dress, or an agreement is reached and certain times and places are agreed. Some wives give grudging permission to go to an occasional meeting, or an occasional weekend in the family caravan. They go into another room, or say "Don't do it when I'm around". Such a TV's wife may say, "You're going to do this thing, whether I like it or not. Go on, but don't expect me to have anything to do with it!" She makes it plain that any agreement is made under duress and that she is disgusted with the whole idea. This may well turn out to be an uneasy compromise. She hates every minute that he is away; he feels that he is still in the closet. Having found out, the TV's wife may set out to discourage it by all the means available to her, or to express her rejection, by disapproving silences, by sarcastic remarks, or abuse or ridicule, even going as far as to talk about it among relatives and friends.

Some wives do no more than tolerate their husband's cross dressing, or they "humour him". If he only wishes to experience the act of dressing, he may accept this, but if there is the urge to try to experience the feminine ethos, to exercise that hidden part of himself, he will know that a part of him that is important to him, is not accepted and the hurt and frustration will go on.

Conversely, the husband may go on dressing in the full knowledge of his wife, yet still refuse to admit it or talk about it. His wife may, at the beginning, reject it, even despise him, but then come to realise that something important is happening, and be very frightened and confused. She may, then, want to try and accept and help, and be very hurt that she is being shut out of a vital part of his life. This is what happened between Yvonne and myself. She knew of my cross-dressing from early in my marriage, having caught me. Yet, in spite of the evidence, I couldn't accept it. "Me, a sissy boy? A closet queen? Never!" I would not try to find out what it meant to me, for I refused to think about it. If I denied it to myself, how could I talk about it? Little was known about transvestism then, and neither of us had the courage to approach the Beaumont Society. So we went on for twenty five years with this empty space in our relationship. Couples, like we were, try to pretend it doesn't exist, only to be reminded of it by little everyday events, and it lies between them, like a stone in their marriage.

There may be many reasons why one should carry on, either to keep the family together or because of the fear of carrying on alone. So a wife may put up with it and hope it will go away. It won't. Or she tries to pretend it doesn't exist. She may try to deny it, maybe for years on end, not only to herself but also to her husband, but inside she knows it is true. It is a natural protective mechanism, which allows one to push the worry out the way and get on with the rest of one's life. But does it solve anything?

It is often suggested that the TV's dressing has a negative effect on his sex life. Certainly, those men who have been emotionally isolated may find it difficult to give of themselves. If they are fighting against secret dressing, they may divert themselves by concentrating more on their jobs. But the trapped feelings will, themselves, divert attention and energy, both from the job and from their wives and families.

In any marriage, sexuality may decrease for a number of reasons. Each partner is less prepared to take the trouble to be attractive. Each has as much as they can handle in terms of looking after the children, or coping with debt and earning a living. Many businesses, for instance, expect their employees to give them twenty four hours a day commitment, without considering the husband's responsibility to his wife and family. Perhaps it is a mistake to consider a lowered interest in sex as being a particular feature of transvestism, rather than looking it as a general feature of humanity. In other words, many men may become sexually inactive; some of them are TV's.

We have to consider the idea that the cross-dressing is diverting the husband's sexual attention from his wife. If this is the case, then the considerations are the same as if it were really another woman, or a substitute turn-on. In a stale marriage, "Independent sex" can be an easy alternative. How many wives have turned over an old sack in the garden shed and found a cache of sex books? How many more have had to put up with real, as opposed to moral unfaithfulness? It may, indeed, be that the TV's wife may be happy to let him keep his secret pastime. If it genuinely doesn't bother her, it might be a suitable compromise. She may, herself, have lost interest in sex, in which case it might be a convenient outlet for his frustration.

But, if this other "female" half of a husband exists as well, is it possible that, if it was allowed to develop as a social being, a friend of the family, he would be better able to direct his sexual attention back to his wife? Could she cope with this new friend of the family? This solution could be better than, for instance, the use of tranquillisers, in an attempt to suppress the cross-dressing urge. They are likely to remove what sex life may be left and also hamper the husband's efforts to earn a living. If a wife loves her husband, it is said, she loves the whole person, including this "feminine" part. But it seems important for the two to be separate, he should be either one or the other. While developing his female self it might be a good idea to encourage his masculine side, including pride in his abilities, and revitalised interest in being a lover. I don't feel it is possible to settle for a middle course. I sometimes catch wives looking at me and I wonder if they are thinking "I hope my husband doesn't get to be like Jed!", at least I hope they do.

Many TV's enjoy a perfectly normal and fulfilling sexual relationship and can't understand why they still feel the need, from time to time, to cross-dress. Most wives and husbands do not take the other person into bed with them. Unless they are in the grip of a fantasy, most husbands see themselves as men making love to women and go to bed as men. A wife may well feel degraded to think that her husband needs props in order to be aroused. She may feel upset at the idea that she can only make love as a lesbian.

This subject is frequently brought up by TV's wives, but occasionally one hears of a TV whose wife is all too accepting and wants to turn it into a bedtime game. These wives have totally misunderstood the situation. I have examined sexual issues, because they are important to many TV's, but equally many TV's do not want to be physically women, they delight in their prowess in bed as men. What they are asking for, is to experience the feminine world.

However, many couples find ways of improving their love life with various aids, chosen together, with love. The permutations are infinite, as is the range of motives on both sides, and, in fact, the couple may feel able to make use of transvestism's erotic aspects. If it is truly acceptable to both partners, the TV may well be able to resolve his problems in sexual expression, and the couple may able to add a fillip to their lovemaking. Some couples make love after a cross-dressing episode, but after taking everything off, as if going to bed. Others may agree on a certain fetish object, such as an item of underwear. The choice is up to the couple concerned, but both must be aware of the needs of the other, and neither must ask the other to do something that they cannot.

There is the true cautionary tale of John and Jane. John was a TV who lived with his partner Mary. She knew of his cross-dressing, to become Jane, when they met and, as a fetishist herself, she enjoyed erotic dressing with him. But she never fully understood either it or him. It is possible that, while Mary welcomed John the fetishist, she was afraid of Jane the transvestite and, in the end, the relationship foundered.

Both partners need to be alert to what the other really wants, and be aware of each other's limits from moment to moment. The husband may want to go further than his wife. She may follow, because it pleases him, but not be entirely happy. The reverse may also happen; in many aspects of sex, one partner may "fake it" out of love for the other.

I hope that divorce is not the inevitable next step. So many divorces are long and bitter affairs. There may well be the urge to make him pay through the nose for what he has done. They are valid feelings and they are important. But, particularly if there is a family, should the feelings of others be disregarded? Only one group of persons gains from a divorce, and it doesn't always include either the plaintiff or the defendant.

If a mutual agreement, including custody arrangements for the children, can be reached before the case ever reaches the courts, or even before a solicitor is consulted, not only money, but a great deal of grief and stress will be saved. Usually, the grounds are published as "behaviour". A plea has to be entered regarding the husband's transvestism, but this is a matter of court record and is not usually made public.

There are, however, many couples who are still together, working things out together. A wife can probably never totally accept it, or fully understand, but many have found ways of accommodating it in the marriage. In most cases, the husbands say that the dressing is not a sexual thing. Perhaps, unconsciously or consciously, these husbands have already made the separation of their two motives, erotic and gender, and directed their sexual attention back to their wives.

In the end, compromise is the name of the game, a joint compromise; two people working together to set guidelines that cause the minimum distress to both, where both parties may even gain some benefit, even a joint interest.

Chapter 15
THE OTHER WOMAN

A young TV once showed me a very private memo he'd written to himself. He said he'd written it at half past three one morning in a fit of rage and frustration, against himself and the world. It was about how he could achieve peace of mind for himself, while not distressing his supportive wife, who he loved very dearly. But in it were all the thoughts and emotions of hundreds of other TV's.

Some couples "cope" with the husband's transvestism, some incorporate it as an intrinsic, shared feature of their marriages. While much of this chapter is about how they go about it, it also highlights some of the problems that may arise.

Almost all TV's, in their preoccupation at the beginning, are unbelievably narcissistic and self-centred. The first thing that is likely to happen is that the husband, finding freedom at last, will go right over the top. Once everything is out in the open, he feels everything in the garden is lovely. It could almost be called a second crisis. He dresses as often as possible, he visits one meeting after another and over-indulges in every way. In a way he is like a man with a new hobby, though it is hardly likely that his wife will see herself as being on a par with a golf widow.

Every TV goes through this period, totally self-centred, preoccupied with the stereotype, the image of the woman he has in his mind. The hardest thing to bear, will be if he constantly indulges in preening and self-admiration in every available mirror. If the marriage itself is secure, sooner or later he calms down. It isn't just the novelty wearing off. Somewhere a compromise is found between what he sees as his need and the value of his everyday life, particularly his marriage.

"Fantastic Women", by Annie Woodhouse, gives several examples of TV's who went straight into Fantasy-Land. They seemed to be saying, "I can't help the way I am, so I can do what I like". But, even if people can't help the way they are, they can help the way they act.

Often such a TV says that he loves his wife and doesn't want to lose her, but allows his cross-dressing to go on without thought. Even if there are agreements, he persistently breaks them. His wife may support him, even actively help him, but, because he is not really considering her, he is not giving her any chance to meet him halfway.

He may buy the most extravagant clothes, such that his wife couldn't afford in six month's saving. A few, still in their fantasy world, build up massive collections, say, of hundreds of pairs of high heeled shoes. He will probably dress too young, or like "mutton dressed up as lamb". In a way it is like having a teenage daughter, dressing up, seeking approval and admiration, visions of being the belle of the ball, the centre of attraction. Yet it is a time when the wife can have the most influence, guiding and helping.

As one TV said in the Derby Evening Telegraph, "I was like a little boy who had been given a bag of sweets." In this case, his wife put her foot down, he had the sense to come down to earth, and they remain married and deeply in love.

He says "My wife is my girlfriend and my best friend". She says "I have the best of both worlds, a strong and loving man, and an affectionate best friend". This is something to hold on to. If he can be all the man you wanted most of the time, he can perhaps be your best friend sometimes, in a special kind of sharing.

There was another TV who, just after he came out, would come home from work every evening, get dressed and do the cooking, the ironing and cleaning. In the end, his wife threatened to pack her bags; she couldn't see that there was any more need for her. It has to be said, that it galls some wives that some TV's will only do the washing up when dressed. On the other hand, some wives may be up to the neck in housework, feeling that they look like nothing on earth, while their TV husbands are pottering around in their finery.

In the beginning, this other being may remain insidiously in the husband's male life. He may go on wearing tights or silky lingerie under his male clothes, or he may keep his varnished toenails. He may leave his female clothes lying around, his nightie hung on the bathroom door. Thus his wife never has "him" alone, to herself. "She" is always lingering around, just barely visible. "She" is always in his thoughts.

He may wish to shave himself from head to foot and this is unlikely to be acceptable. Perhaps there is room for a bargain. For instance, the TV may agree to shave only those parts that show, hands and lower legs. Many couples have an agreement that the husband should keep his chest hair, at least. With an agreement to express his female side, it is only fair that he should maintain his male side. Most couples have a mutually recognised signal when the TV wants to be his other self. Perhaps he will say "Jane would like to come for a visit", and if his wife says that she doesn't want her to, on that occasion, that is the end of the matter.

There has to come a time when he says to himself, "Do I really love my wife?", "Do I love her because she is complaisant, or because I want us to share our lives?", "Does my femme half really relate to her as a woman might?", "Am I letting myself become too preoccupied with it all?", "Isn't there something of value in my male role?", "Do I really want to be a second class citizen?", "Do I only do the dishes when I'm dressed, or as a genuine wish to help?", "Does she really like to go to bed with me when I have no body hair and I'm wearing a nightie?", "Would I let her go out with me if she were wearing a ratting cap and hob-nailed boots?", "Is transvestism really a oneness with women, or is it stealing their space, an example of men's lack of real concern for women?" These are all questions that have been suggested by various women in TV's lives.

Some TV's, even though their wives are trying to be supportive, make the mistake of only part dressing, or possibly from a hangover of the guilt of it all, cannot bring themselves to dress completely. For a husband to sit in his normal clothes, except that he has a skirt on, maybe even smoking a pipe, is almost always extremely distressing for his wife. Often I see such couples as desperately hanging on to the status quo, yet the wife must feel that she is living with a time-bomb. He may be afraid of "letting go", feeling, possibly, that the urge may take over. Often he wears little or no ornamentation as a man. While encouragement in this direction may help, he may be feeling that the male image has no value to him, that it has reached an impasse.

I think it is important to do the job properly. A transvestite's wife is almost always more at ease with the total image of the other woman. Interestingly, we pirated a copy of the television programme, Hodgson Confidential, for study by the Wives and Partners Group. Near the beginning, it shows transvestites changing their clothes before a meeting. Not only our TV's wives, but the TV's themselves, found this upsetting. People can feel comfortable with viewing the two persona as two different people and are uncomfortable with half and half.

In just the same way, the general public have become accustomed to transexuals to an extent, but still are unable to accept "part time women" - people who appear in one guise one day and another the next.

As already suggested, a wife can often help in the creation of this other image, and it often helps both partners to do so. Few TV's fresh from the closet dress convincingly. An important study, is the practice of authentic feminine gestures, providing they are not overdone, and in learning to walk like a lady. One TV told the author that his wife had made him walk up and down for over an hour, until she was satisfied. He said, "I was exhausted, but I felt that it was well worthwhile, and we both felt the joy of doing something together".

Women walk the way they do partly because of their physique, which men don't share. Most men are fairly tall. I rarely wear high heels, because of the danger of concussion on the tops of doorways! The increase in the number of tall women in recent years has been a boon to TV's. Not only are they less conspicuous, but there is an increasing range of stylish clothes and shoes in the larger sizes, especially in mail order catalogues.

Quite often, the TV's wife will help in building her husbands's wardrobe, either offering helpful suggestions or enjoying being consulted about the choice of clothing and accessories. A change of tastes may be offered by pointing out fashion trends and complimenting him on his appearance. Many cross-dressers have good taste, but some lean towards being "tarty". If both are close to the same size, they could remember Joan River's dictum: "If you want to increase your wardrobe, marry a transvestite!" Some couples never wear each other's clothes, some do swap, but never without asking permission. Many wives shop for their cross-dressing spouse or with him, or contribute by sewing, which insures a good fit and keeps the cost down. It is said that a woman's crowning glory is her hair, and the effect of a good wig, well styled, is dramatic. But few men know how to take care of long hair, especially if it is in the form of a wig.

There must come a point when a wife will ask herself how "she" relates to her, as a woman and a wife? As a rival to her as a woman? As a rival for his affections? Or as a good friend and comrade. It is important for her to be sure about this in her mind, but it is a learning process for both husband and wife.

The effect of the change in image may be startling, or have unpredictable effects. One wife said that she was amazed at how pretty this other image of her husband was, and felt she had to compete, not only for his affections, but in appearance as well. Others feel that making themselves look pretty is a means of continuing the courtship into the marriage and lose interest, feeling that they shouldn't bother any more. Somehow the TV has penetrated the mysteries of how his wife makes herself attractive for him and appropriated them. Problems can also arise if the TV's wife is over-supportive and the TV feels smothered in the development of his other self, or he might find that she is, herself, competing for attention at social gatherings.

It may be that she tries to build in attributes that she would like for herself. I used the analogy of guiding a teenage daughter. Often, a husband's other half may need to grow as a female person in her own right, not as an image of his wife, or any other woman. But the attributes that he sees in his other half are likely to be the very attributes he saw in his wife, when he married her. It may be that the friendship between his wife and this strange other woman may grow all the more close. At the same time, the husband should not allow his male image deteriorate and they could work together on this as well. It might be no bad idea if he put on his best suit and took his wife out to dinner, from time to time, making sure that "he" is all "him".

Often, a more established TV may not want to go through the whole rigmarole of changing, and complains that his wife can slop about in old clothes as she wants. The idea of wearing jeans and jumper, except that they are women's ones, may be acceptable as a compromise, or a candlewick, instead of a "manly" dressing gown, providing that it is clear that it is a genuine cross-dressing session. At a meeting, a wife commented on the fact that TV's were always very smart. It was gently pointed out that a woman can wear casual clothes, because she already looks like one.

I said at the beginning that this is a book of ideas, and questions. These two chapters have offered a series of options. Acceptance is probably the most real and urgent need for a TV. The wife who accepts most will be the one who loves most, but she won't be a doormat. It will be conditional acceptance, which will require that he has a regard for her feelings as well. A TV's wife is a person herself. She has emotions and prejudices built into her own personality. If disclosure has come about by discovery, or by a ham-fisted disclosure, there will be a lot of bridges to build. If he can demonstrate his love for her by waiting, with a gentle opening out of his feelings to her, she may be able to acknowledge her love for the whole of him, warts and all. She may never be able to stomach the idea of her husband in a dress, still less actually see him cross-dressed. She may never be completely happy about it, and may well wish that he had picked some other preoccupation, but she may come to accept that it is an avenue that he must explore. It may be that the TV, replacing guilt with conscience and sensitivity for the feelings of others, with the worst part of the secrecy gone, and with the loving support of his wife, can exercise discretion and temperance in his cross-dressing.

It isn't a one way street as far as the TV's wife is concerned. She doesn't become the female stereotype, the loving wife helping her husband in his adversity. On a practical level, if it were considered a hobby, it needn't separate him from her, as so many do. It is a shared thing, and she might take pride in helping to create the female him, as she takes pride in the male him. Many wives go further than this. Both partners put aside all negative feelings of guilt and rejection, and work together, talking about what it means to them. While his wife realises that it brings pleasure to him, which will benefit her, he sets out to build his "woman" into the sort of person she would pick as a friend, and she sets out to get to know this friend. Some couples say that "him" and "her" disappear, they are but two facets of the same person. So often, in "ordinary" marriages, the husband and wife only relate on the physical plane. The degree of empathy between a TV and his wife is often so much closer; they have a genuine concern for each other as persons. In working together to explore this new person, they get to know more about each other. In finding out about his feminine side, the husband comes to appreciate his wife's femininity all the more.

The suggestion is that, as the TV is able to express his whole self, so his wife finds herself free to do so also. As he develops as a whole person, so does his wife, and they both seem to grow closer together. As I write this, I can't help feeling that this is the real meaning of the Chinese Yin-Yang symbol, so beloved of TV's. Many TV's wives that I have met seem exquisitely feminine, yet you feel they could throw their weight around, if they wanted to. One wife suggested that a TV has a much greater capacity for loving, because it is in their nature. Another TV said "How can we ever lie to each other again, when we have shared ourselves so deeply?" Again, on a more practical level, the TV understands his wife's occasional need to go out and buy herself something pretty and new. Many TV's and their wives go out shopping for clothes together, not necessarily with him "dressed". Many have said that, being so at ease with the idea, they have embarrassed themselves by discussing potential purchases out loud. But no-one worries, anyone within earshot is likely to be pleased to share the joke.

A question that is frequently asked is whether the children should be told about it, and at what age. As with everything connected with this complicated subject, it depends on the family involved. Some say it is wrong to continue the deception, or wrong to lie to one's children. Practically everyone who has set out to advise on the subject, however, suggests that the reasons, why one shouldn't tell, outweigh all others. All I can give are the pro's and cons.

There are cases nowadays of "changed over" transexuals rearing children. The fear is that very young children will become confused at a time when they are still learning about gender roles. There is, of course, a difference between knowing about it, perhaps as a dressing up game, and seeing the father regularly switching roles. My personal feeling is that they find out more about themselves and their relationship to others and Society from other children of their own age. Perhaps it could be said that grown-ups are different, they provide an aim for the future, not for the present, they have already "grown up", the family provides security, a safe harbour for the child to return to, after his expeditions into the world. I have always been in favour of well-run playgroups for all children (not only those of TV's!) to expose them to as wide a range of role models as possible. All parents have all sorts of quirks, although they may be unaware of them, and the sooner a child is absorbed into childhood society the better. When the other children's emotional patterns have not become fixed either, then the child who is "different" is more easily absorbed; in effect, they are all learning together.

More importantly, to a child, anything his parents do is right. I was nine or ten before I realised that my father was different in that he had an artificial leg! So Daddy likes to wear a dress sometimes, how are you going to explain to the child that he, or she, mustn't talk about it. How do you lay a secret like that on a child?

Children are very good at finding things out that they aren't meant to. They may wonder why there are size 8 shoes in the wardrobe, when Mummy takes size 5, and think little about it. But it would be a different matter if they accidentally saw Daddy dressed.

Teenagers nowadays treat it much more casually then we did, thanks to David Bowie, Boy George et al, but you have to remember that they have little experience of real people and think in terms of a set of stereotypes, father, mother, teacher and so on. Neither boys nor girls have experienced the infinite variety of real people. They may find it hard to discover that father is not the person they have always known. Moreover, a son will be struggling to find his own manhood and his place in Society.

If I were pressed, I would suggest a time when the children were old enough to understand why some families have secrets that they don't talk about outside, without it appearing a big thing to them, yet before they grow up into teenage to have to start sorting out their own identities.

I think one must be sure, in not telling the children, that it is not out of guilt, but discretion. I feel that is important that the husband and wife should have come to some sort of agreement. Children are very sensitive to stress in the relationship of their parents. If the truth slips out, they will be put in the position of having to take sides.

There may also be problems if, for instance, the transvestite dies with the children not knowing. One solution is to inform a close friend, possibly asking him to be one's executor, who could clear away that part of one's life. Another idea might be to leave a letter explaining matters.

As for youngsters under eighteen, if one approaches a helpline or group, especially with transvestism being such a sensitive subject, the helpline will tend to feel uncomfortable, if parents or guardians are not involved. However, transvestite helping organisations are increasingly being consulted by professional agencies. Hopefully, this trend will continue, and the reaction will become increasingly supportive, for teenage is probably the most difficult and confused time for anyone. Maybe it will be possible for a young TV to approach professional help and perhaps the professional will allow a TV helpline worker to attend.

It may be difficult, if you find your son dressing up, to react calmly, but to reinforce guilt feelings that are already present, can only exacerbate later problems. Punishment does not seem to make any difference. A number of TV's have told stories of being caught by their parents and given a good hiding. One told me that his father had, on one occasion, broken two of his ribs. But they went on dressing.

Chapter 16
OUT AND ABOUT

One day, I went to the front door to let the cat out, and there, walking past, was a transvestite. It was probably the best time and place; midday Saturday in a small market town, with plenty of people around, too busy shopping to do more than smile, after he went by. For he was "read" by just about everyone. The main trouble was that he was wearing high heels, but still taking big strides. His lips were set in a thin line of nervousness, and he was walking in a stooped, defensive posture. If he had met some youths who took a dislike to him, it might have been a different story.

I guess that there would have been no stopping him, but I wanted to say "Get off to a club, where you can get your act together in safety. There are places in this country, where TV's are accepted and can go out and about. Why not behave as if you are enjoying yourself. Walk straight but relaxed, and act as if it were the most natural thing in the world. If you think that there is something shameful about what you are doing, so will everyone else."

Sooner or later, nearly every TV begins to feel restricted by the confines of his bedroom; "all dressed up and nowhere to go!" He seeks to 'extend his closet', at first to the whole of his house, then to go out in public, as any woman can.

It should be said that, where there is an erotic element, as familiarity with the closet diminishes the excitement, it may also be part of the temptation to indulge in more advanced adventures. But the closet TV, venturing forth for the first time, has no idea of how to act in a feminine manner. Even if dressed respectably, he is likely to draw attention. He is also likely to go abroad late at night, at a time when no woman would dare to be out alone.

A possible scenario is that the police pull up beside him in their panda car, either to ask what he is doing, or wondering why a lady is walking down the street at that time of night. If he takes fright and runs away, the police naturally give chase. As they try to stop him, he may well panic and struggle. Normally they might have just taken him home, for safety, but now it is a case of assault.

The Police attitude is usually laissez-faire. It is not specifically against the law, except for possible local bye-laws. The usual charge is the common law one of "behaviour liable to cause a breach of the peace", the interpretation of which, in court, is unpredictable. A man dressed as a woman is a nuisance in the cells, and having to take time in court to give evidence is a something that the Police can well do without. Some of the more macho policemen will have a bit of fun with the TV before they let him go. On the other hand, a friend of mine, a pre-op TS, was stopped, one night, for a traffic offence. She quietly explained who she was and what she was about. The officer took it in his stride and was good enough to call her "Madam" throughout the interview.

To quote from the Gender Trust's "Guide to Transexualism":

"It is not illegal to dress in the clothes of the other gender. But, under Common Law, a charge of Breach of the Peace could be made."

"A charge could be (and has been) brought by a Police Officer following an arrest for conduct likely to cause a breach of the peace. The offender could be 'bound over to keep the peace' or fined on subsequent offences."

"The Sexual Offences Act 1956 (Sect. 32) might be applied if the (unthinking) M to F TS (or TV) were out in a place of prostitution, or if seen waiting around, dressed provocatively."

While the above is true, in general, I would be wary of local bye-laws. Other possible charges, under common law could 'offensive and disgusting behaviour', 'open lewdness', 'whatever outrages decency'. The police do not have to show that anyone was actually offended, only that they could be. These comments have been 'lifted' from Forum, Vol 24, No. 8, page 94, which also mentions the Public Order Act of 1986, which requires the Police to prove that the TV intended 'insulting', or 'disorderly' behaviour, in a public place, or was aware that it could be considered as such.

A great many TV's do go out and about in public, and do so rarely detected. To be "read" is a failure. There is, of course, a challenge in going out and "passing" as a woman. While there may be the spice of danger, and the fun of fooling people, the overwhelming motivation is for this "other self" to be accepted. The public, in general, is tolerant and I feel, strongly, that if they are willing to allow us our idiosyncrasy, then we should try not to give offence.

Experienced TV's follow certain rules of discretion as to the time and the place. This is particularly so in regard to the major problem of toilet facilities. Public toilets are virtually "no go" areas, for obvious reasons. You can imagine the reaction of a man on entering a toilet and finding a 'woman' there. The result may well be a charge of soliciting. Similarly, however tolerant women may be, they are not likely to be pleased to find that their one private place has been invaded. The immediate assumption is that the TV is some kind of pervert.

"Coming out" is a lonely process. You want somebody to tell you what you should do and where you should go, but there is no-one in the world who knows you well enough. You have to do it all yourself, but it helps to be with others in the same position. There are meetings held in towns and cities all over the country which a TV might like to visit. Many are held in council-run premises and community centres. Others are held in gay pubs and clubs, those that will accept TV's. Several times a year, weekend holidays are organised in perfectly ordinary hotels.

To attend what, from the outside, appears to be an esoteric secret society, for the first time is a daunting prospect. It is a safe place to "extend the closet", although it isn't compulsory to wear a dress. For the first few times, one can go in male clothes, just to see what goes on. Most TV's travel in their male clothes and usually there are changing facilities of one sort or another. Such meetings are strictly social affairs. The atmosphere is of a group of human beings who are all in the same boat. They are somewhat daunting to someone who feels he has not practised the image sufficiently well, but there are tacit agreements. No-one will comment adversely on another's appearance, or offer gratuitous advice on personal matters.

Security is also paramount. No-one will ask questions about another's private life, if information is not volunteered. In this context it is as well to choose a "femme name", a nom de guerre, which will protect one's real identity. Very few TV's use their real name in public. If they appear in the press, or on TV, they keep their family name secret. Those that attend meetings travel in their male clothes near their home territory.

Everyone is completely anonymous. Even if there is someone present that one knows, as happened to me, one should remember that they have just as much to hide as anyone else by careless talk. A point of etiquette is that one refers to someone as "she" if wearing a dress, or "he" if wearing a suit!

These meetings are not a place for sexual contacts. If the TV is looking for this, he may well find a friend, and may form a friendship, but anyone who goes with overt sexual intent will be quietly shown the door.

Learning to put on makeup is a salutary exercise. Maybe for the first time, the TV has to accept that it is a man's face, and his face, not the image of the woman that he sees himself as.

The beginner almost always overdoes it, as if putting on a disguise. Oddly enough, the trick is not to try and make one's self look like a woman, but to study the face, like a woman does, and decide on the good points and the bad points.

The first step is to have the closest possible shave, a real case of blood, sweat and tears. I put Savlon cream on my face afterwards. It soothes the skin and, as I find the bits that I've missed, it lubricates the razor while I fetch them off. This could be a good tip for any male reader, if he's planning to go out on a special date! There are various preparations for covering scars and other marks, which will hide any remaining beard shadow, and can be obtained from any chemist. Some dry on the skin, but remain flexible, which stops them from rubbing off onto clothes.

Another mistake the beginner makes is to wear impossibly high heels. While they may be alright in the closet, they need a lot of practice to wear safely when negotiating a wide range of surfaces. In any case, if one has a car, a pair of flat shoes should be kept for driving. Apart from the safety aspect, the Police may consider that one is not in proper control of the car, a line they sometimes take with lady drivers. For an ordinary meeting, the TV should dress down rather than up, at least at first. A simple blouse and a flared or pleated skirt (below the knee) is best, rather than a dress. A short jacket, cardigan, or peplum, will help to hide the lack of a figure. Usually, if the blouse is patterned, the skirt should be plain, or vice versa. As I said in a previous chapter, most novice TV's dress too young, and to the image they have in their minds. They learn what every woman learns; to dress as she is and not as she wishes she were. There is no way a middle-aged woman can look like a teenage girl, for instance. It helps to bring one back to earth.

Everybody arriving at their first meeting, wonders what they are going to find on the other side of the door; perhaps rows of pouting, powdered, camp 'females', like pantomime dames. They wonder if they'll find themselves in a strange underworld of exotic sexual practices. They make a dozen false approaches, hang around outside for an hour working up their nerve. Everybody remembers their first meeting, how they, finally, took a deep breath and, metaphorically shutting their eyes, plunged in through the door.

What I found is a tremendous friendship and sympathy, and humanity. No-one puts up a 'front', everyone is able be their real selves; and I was able to relax and express a part of myself that I'd kept subdued for so long. The variation is endless. There are beginners who have not quite "got it together" and there are others who are quite content just to throw on a dress and a shapeless wig. You can see some who, after many years, still feel a little embarrassed about it all. Some are quite at home, but are content to be "men in dresses", moving about chatting. Some are quite open about their fantasies, with fifties circular skirts or mini dresses and four inch heels. Most, however, set out to put on a womanly image as completely as possible, according to their age.

No-one should be put off by the fact that some meetings are held in gay venues. As a minority group themselves, many of them allow TV's to use their facilities. One city has a whole gay area. The TV meeting is in the centre of it and members come and go as they please between the various pubs and clubs. Some meetings are held in private houses, many in public community centres.

At one, the domino team, having been ousted by the introduction of a pool table, asked if they might use a corner of the room booked by the TV's. For some years now, TV's and local people have mingled happily, even to joining in the TV's Christmas party. I was chatting to Julie, the centre's manager, a lady, near the end of this event, and she said "You know, I really love these Thursday evenings!" This meeting has been running now for over ten years in the middle of a housing estate and I doubt if it is any great secret. One night, the TV's held a jewellery party. At the end of the Bingo session next door, several of the ladies came in to look over the jewellery.

Most wives experience the problems of secrecy themselves. They are fearful of friends casually dropping in, and it restricts their social lives. They become frightened to even talk to people, in case they "know". They may become very sensitive about their husband's shaved legs, when they wear shorts, or their families go swimming. They are often afraid that the husband might become careless, or want to be more open in public. Women, naturally, have been learning to "be" women in public all their lives, and it has become "second nature" for them. Most TV's take the biggest risks at the beginning, when there may be an air of recklessness, the urge to challenge, to establish a right to go out as a woman. It is, of course, their wives who have to live with the neighbours.

The loneliness of a wife facing the fact of her husband's transvestism approaches that of the closet TV himself. Who can she talk to, apart from her husband? He, at the beginning, may, himself, not know much about what he wants and what is driving him.

The Women of the Beaumont Society, a group which has the unlovely acronym of WOBS, has three special phonelines, operated by transvestites wives, and wives assist in the running of the Trans-Net helpline.

Some of the other helping groups for wives seem to deal with the wife's point of view in isolation. The Wives' and Partner's Groups in various parts of the country, place the emphasis on the two sorting it out as a couple. "Fantastic Women" includes an account of a meeting at the TV/TS centre in London, which describes the wives sitting in one room grumbling about the men, while the men are in another room ignoring the women. There are other groups around the country who seem to be saying "We must do something about the little women", as though it can give them an excuse. Thus they find it incomprehensible that the one rule of the Derbyshire Wive's and Partner's meetings, launched by Trans-Net, is that the TV himself must attend in his male clothes.

But it works. The husband and wife are nervous enough about meeting others for the first time, without the prospect of seeing men dressed as women. The meetings are quiet affairs, just coffee evenings,with the difference that they are the one place where the subject can be talked about openly.

At first most wives, even if they can come to tolerate it in their husbands, cannot face the idea of meeting anyone else. But when they meet other couples in the same circumstance and share their feelings with them, they may begin to feel that they are not completely on their own. Talking things through may help to put them into perspective. Some very close friendships have been formed in this way. There is something in common and the wives give each other support.

Some couples form close friendships, visit each other and socialise generally, others prefer to remain isolated. There are plenty of "dress" meetings that the husband can attend, if and when he feels the need, and wives are usually welcomed. Generally, if they accompany their TV husbands to meetings, they feel more comfortable with those that are a considerable distance from their home territory. There are various weekend meetings held in hotels around the country. At one, recently, the press sent reporters who, unfortunately arrived too late. Since nobody would tell them anything, they made up their own stories. The result was that many of the town's shopkeepers and the occupants of houses neighbouring the hotel, wrote to the hotel in support of the TV's. In fact, the hotel staff usually enjoy these weekends. They are great fun, everyone is happy and there is no rowdiness.

Chapter 17
THE WELL-ADJUSTED TV

Most TV's, after their initial fling, begin to think about their real problems, the ones that lie parallel to their gender motivation.

I certainly feel that before I came out, I was living like a zombie; just existing from minute to minute, unconsciously hiding from the feelings inside me. I worked all hours and, when I wasn't working, I was busy repairing the house. Admittedly, with four children, we didn't have much money, and I had to do the jobs myself. Was I a workaholic? (Am I now?). I didn't consciously hide away from myself but apparently my wife had once commented to my mother that I seemed to live in a world of my own. I have to say that "coming out" didn't have the result I expected, for I certainly didn't become the vivacious and lively person I was certain was inside me, the life and soul of every party. At parties, I'm still the eternal wallflower and I couldn't venture onto a dance floor to save my life. Inside every introvert is an extrovert fighting to get out!

Often, when I get an idea like that, I find myself playing around with it, and I couldn't help wondering if, while I escape by being an introvert, some people escape by being extrovert. Perhaps they may be so busy projecting themselves outwards, they ignore, or refuse to consider what is going on inside them, including factors affecting their physical well-being. I wonder if the ideal way to be, is a suitable mixture of both introvert and extrovert?

Sooner or later, many TV's review their complete lifestyle. Most TV's realise that their male life-style is the more important to them. One has to look clearly at one's self and what is valuable in one's life. Particularly, if one is thinking of changing over, one has to be sure that the emotions one feels really have surfaced out of the past, and are not those one would like to have to fit one's new self. One may moderate one's masculine role, where it is has been particularly aggressive; one might have been going to excess and being hyper-macho. Thus, in developing one's female half, one may develop the male half to become a more mature and controlled male role. One TV even told me that it had improved his game of Rugby! He felt that, before, he had literally been going out and looking for a fight. With less need to dissipate what he felt might be unnecessary aggression, he felt that he played just as tough a game, but devoted more attention to the tactics.

Since their conflict is with the role that they feel Society has dictated, TV's have the urge to seek Society's approval for what they are, and not what they're supposed to be, by talking about it to people outside of the family. This is often a major worry for TV's wives. The thought of family and friends discovering the secret is absolutely frightening, with the fear of ridicule and rejection.

In a sense, the TV sets out, by careful disclosure, to create an environment in which he can live with peace of mind. The extent of this varies from one TV to another. One can be content with only his wife knowing, while another needs to disclose to his immediate colleagues at work. Generally, I think it is the husband who is secure in his wife's and family's love that can restrict his profile to the family. It is single TV's that seem to need to be more "open" about themselves.

Certainly it seems to be factor in seeking surgery. Peggy J.Rudd, in "My Husband Wears my Clothes", quotes a survey, where the question was asked "Would you have surgery if you could afford the costs?" While some said that they would, a good many more said that they wouldn't, and about 25% left the question open. Most of those, that said that they would, also shared stories of rejection.

I have come very much into the open to try and shed some light onto the situation, to help those in the position that Yvonne and I were in. But it helps me as well. The words "I am a transvestite" are an affirmation of myself. On the surface, they mean I wear women's clothes. But they mean much, much more and as I find more and more people who can accept me as I am, so the feelings involved are more contained.

However, there are many people who have a public position to maintain. They may be managers or foremen, soldiers or policemen and a change in attitude is out of the question. If, for instance, the TV is a coal miner, disclosure could cause someone to take a dislike to him and drop a pit prop on him. The TV's management may well disapprove and he could lose his job.

It was interesting to see, in a Sunday paper, a feature about a man who had decided to live and work totally as a woman. The article included a photograph, was sympathetic and made it clear that he regarded himself as a heterosexual transvestite.

To do this, requires a long period of preparation. I was known as a transvestite to many of my company's directors and colleagues, (though I volunteered the promise not to arrive at work in a dress!). There was a period of awkwardness before I was accepted, and it helped that I had already worked for a number of years with the company. Unfortunately, there are those who take it into their heads to simply turn up for work, dressed as women, and then are deeply hurt at the reaction. This has happened in a number of cases with transexuals.

Transvestites tend to seek acceptance by Society, on their own terms, rather than Society's. They consistently look at

Society from their own point of view, rather than from the other direction. In any case, no-one who has not fully accepted himself or, at least, come to terms with himself, can expect anyone else to accept him.

This conflict with Society and the TV's lifestyle, produces an urge to escape; to get away to somewhere where the TV can be as he wants to be. There are many transvestites living alone as virtual recluses. In "A Man's Tale", by John Pepper, the author finished up in a commune. A female to male TS, Michael Dillon, became a Buddhist monk. There are hundreds more, living quietly by themselves, keeping to themselves. This isn't, of course, solely a transvestite phenomenon. Many people say that, at some time in their lives, all they have wanted to do was to dig a hole in the ground, jump in and pull the earth over their head.

The three major stresses have gone, however; the stress of guilt, the stress of secrecy and the stress of wanting to dress and feeling unable to. The obsession reduces to a compulsion, then to a need. With freedom to dress more often, the TV reaches the point where he dresses only when he feels he needs the escape.

Sometimes a transvestite will stop dressing altogether, which may not be a good thing; it depends on the reason. The one least likely to succeed is where the TV decides to give it up, like giving up smoking.

A very common reason for stopping dressing is dissatisfaction with the results. But, however far you go in changing yourself, it is always your own eyes that look back at you from the mirror. You still need to use a little fantasy. You have to remember that others are not so familiar with your face as you are.

Alternatively, what clothing one wears becomes irrelevant, thus the male and female image disappear and one is left in the middle. Interestingly, many TV's, with full freedom to dress, report a curious hesitation at the last minute, a resistance to dropping the male image.

On the other hand, having come completely to terms with himself, and worked out what it means for him, a TV can stop for a while, for instance, if it would cause distress or embarrassment to someone. Thus, where the children "don't know", with stresses gone and the loving support of his wife, the TV can more easily limit himself to special times and places. Perhaps these may be the regular TV meeting, or periods in the family caravan. The need to dress or, for that matter, to change over, is reduced if one can direct one's emotional needs in other ways, or if one can improve one's life skills.

Often there will appear signs of strain between a TV and his wife who seem to have been perfectly happy for years. What is happening? Often it is the bane of all marriages; one taking the other for granted. There may be the feeling, even after many years, that their husband might want to go further. Both partner's feelings will vary from day to day. She may feel that it is taking up too much time, or attention, or money. She may feel that her social life is starting to revolve around TV meetings. He might become careless about removing make-up, he might borrow her favourite clothes without her permission, he might use her dressing table and leave it untidy. He may not be showing his appreciation of her as a woman, not only her feminine virtues, but her hard work as well.

If the TV continually displays his idea of womanhood in superficial terms, without acknowledging the daily routine, it is understandable that she will become impatient with his pastime. He may have just come in from work and want to unwind, but his wife will also have spent all day performing the household work. Many wives, in today's economy, go out to work as well, and they have it all to do when they come home. It is a source of puzzled frustration to many wives that all their TV husbands have to do is to slip on a dress and they are immediately relaxed. They wonder how he does it. Sharing includes housework and cleaning, and a sharing, but not competing, in domestic interests. Perhaps the TV could put on his jumper and jeans, and give a hand, then both could settle down and relax.

Most TV's are fairly chauvinistic as men, which might not be a bad thing. Is it possible that, if their male side became more feminine, it might also become less masculine? It is important for a man to have that drive and assertiveness, and pride in his abilities, not only for his wife, but in order to function effectively as a man.

At a workshop during a conference in Manchester, I was struck by a comment that appeared in the transcript of it, where a TV's wife had suggested, somewhat wistfully, that surely a man could express himself in a feminine way without dressing up. Why swap one stereotype for another? I suppose he could, but it wouldn't be the same. Somehow, in order to shake off his male side, for a while, he has to switch right over and leave it behind.

There are many men who have qualities that are gentle, caring, mild mannered, all the qualities that one associates with women, yet they have never thought of themselves as feminine or female. Perhaps, when we were young, there was a switch that said "man", after all, but it took no regard of emotional characteristics, so that the TV had to create an alternative role to exercise some of them. Or it may be simply be that the switch, if there is one, is an over-strong sense of gender differences, a susceptibility to being what one is told: "You are a man, therefore you behave in such a way".

From Jung, through to Money, successive psychologists have asserted that every man has the elements of the feminine, and every woman has elements of the masculine. But what is masculine and feminine? Why should each gender have an exclusive prerogative on certain feelings and emotions? Is it that we define the roles too narrowly? Some men can express all their feelings naturally in their lives. Why is it that some fight them, or have to express them in two separate persona?

TV wives do, at times, urge their husbands to be more exotic in their choice of clothes, as though they feel, maybe rightly, that they are getting a bit too serious about it all. While most TV husbands set out to be realistic in their portrayal of their "other part", some can follow their fancy in dressing, especially for parties. Many TV's like to dress, from time to time, in the fashions of their youth, for instance, the peasant blouses and circular skirts, with the multi-tiered waist slips of their youth. One regularly appears in the full rock and roll costume, another in vinyl or satin, with eyelashes that fan you with their breeze, to the consternation of the more staid TV's. Another that I know, is an excellent seamstress himself and makes clothes for his wife, and other TV's and their wives. For himself (or herself), his inventiveness in terms of costume and make-up has turned it into an art form.

There is, in all people, the urge to tell others about themselves. A quiet, shy man might exercise the extrovert in himself, by allowing his female half to be a little flamboyant, when the occasion is right, and learn to carry it off. I often feel such people are having a quiet joke at their own expense. To quote Donahue, the American television presenter, "Don't worry! Laughter will get us through!"

If the TV and his wife can work on it together as a hobby, even a shared one, it can become a role-playing game, a stress reliever, no different, and just as innocent as any other.

Children exercise their intellect and live different experiences by role playing, dressing-up games. When adults, they act out the part of being members of The Sealed Knot, or as Vikings, Wild West characters, jousting knights and so on. It isn't uncommon for men and women to emulate people that they feel an affinity with. Perhaps imitation is the sincerest form of flattery! Part of the relaxation, of course, is from the concentration on one aim, for a while; one that involves all of the senses.

It is never sensible to take any of life's endeavours too seriously. At a conference organised by The Beaumont Trust, there was a workshop entitled "The Well-Adjusted TV". One of the suggestions made, for a suitable attribute, was a sense of humour. The well-adjusted TV says "What a berk I am. But I enjoy life!"

In a less emotive subject, such as sport, one might be a rugby player, a tennis star, a hurdler or a long-distance runner. So different TV's dress in different ways, just as aeromodellers construct their models according to their needs. Some models look nothing like the real thing, but fly beautifully. Other models are built for realism, but will never get off the ground.

Another happily married transvestite that the writer knows, regularly patronises ladies dress and shoe shops, and introduces himself by saying "I lead two very interesting lives". Note that this is a duality of role, not central identity. The conflict will always be there, but now it is managed, not suppressed.

The danger, perhaps, is that in reaching those in trouble, we disturb those who are happy as they are. There are many who find no trouble in dressing, from time to time, in private. If brought out, with promises of glories to come, they might well be worse off. There is a scene in "Young Frankenstein" with Marty Feldman as Igor. The dialogue goes something like this:

The world famous doctor and surgeon says, "I am a world famous doctor and surgeon. I can do something about that hump for you" and Igor says, "What hump?" Many TV's refer to coming out as akin to opening Pandora's Box. Once opened, it can never be closed. The difference is that, with care, maybe, good can come from it. But only the individual concerned can assess the likely result.

I hope that I don't appear to be portraying cross-dressing as something virtuous, and TV's as especially wonderful members of Society. They are just people, like anyone else.

Chapter 18
SELF HELP GROUPS

My personal definition of 'coming out' is those first halting words to another person, whether it is a wife, a friend or a helpline. It is the end of the secrecy and the loneliness.

All over the country, there are telephone helplines. These are expensive to operate, and, being manned by volunteers, are only open for limited hours. Usually they are engaged. The value is that the caller will be, at last, talking to another TV, usually to hear a reassuringly gruff voice, not at all camp or effeminate. Some helplines, it has to be said, simply advise details of meetings, some are ego trips for the operators. But there are a number that are approaching the job in as professional a manner as possible, operated by ex-Samaritans, or trained by The Beaumont Trust.

In the mid-eighties, a TV and his wife were struggling to sort themselves out and make a place, within the love they had for each other, for his strange alter ego. In desperation, he travelled to London to try and find the Beaumont Society. In the end, he phoned a number in the directory, to receive a perplexed reply from the other end. After the fourth attempt to make himself understood, he shouted, "I'm a transvestite!". He was using a kiosk on St. Pancras Station, at the time, and the queue behind took several paces backwards. The number, in fact, was that for a residential home for elderly people. So he wrote a letter, but it was over a year before he became a member. The result was, that the two of them set out to try to help others in the same predicament. Their commitment, to this day, is difficult to express, except to point out that they give it equal priority with their private life. The fact that they keep the line open as nearly permanently as they can, means that they get the crises when they occur.

They were the first of the full time helplines. Crises do not happen conveniently at 7.30 on a Tuesday evening, thus the part-time helplines do not, perhaps, appreciate the full measure of the distress that transvestism can bring.

Quite often the liberation that a TV feels when he "comes out", makes him want to help others, what one consultant calls the "Born-again Christian syndrome". Most established TV's have forgotten what it used to be like for them. One of the most consistent mistakes that they make is the tendency to suggest that the other TV should get about and enjoy life as a TV, forgetting that until someone has fully accepted himself as he is, he is incapable of doing so.

Helplines do not give advice and they only answer questions for which there is a direct factual answer to a direct question, and with care, even then. An example would be the number of another group. Their function is not to promote the operator's, or anyone else's, opinions. One of men's fundamental weaknesses is that they automatically try to cap what is said to them by a comment of their own. The golden rule for a helpline is listen, don't talk. It helps to say "um" or "yes" or "no" to reassure the caller that someone is still there. If it is felt that the caller needs prompting, or one wants to offer an idea, make it a question: "Do you think?", "Do you feel?". Better still, give the caller the option of answering by saying something like, "Would you like to tell me etc." When people operate phonelines from their homes, it is difficult for them to be "present" for the caller, that is, totally with him, or her. It is a good idea to open it at set times, with an Answerphone at others. The mind should be clear of worries about the gas bill, plans to redecorate the back bedroom or the plot of a television play which happens to be showing. While the phone is ringing, the mind should be opened up to the call. Remember that even a trivial call may conceal something serious. While the caller is asking about the nearest meeting place to Bradford, he may want to say that he's on the edge of suicide, but can't find the words. That call may be the positive step that brings him back from the brink, however innocent the content. If the line has been left open, accidentally, on a Bank Holiday, say, don't tell him to call another day. Don't try to work a line alone. If it is being done properly, the operator will be taking other people's emotion on board and it may build up. Colleagues are needed to whom one can unload in confidence.

The foregoing is included for those who feel that they must rush into opening a phoneline to tell the world how good they feel. It would be better if they first spent some time with a regular helpline, like The Samaritans, gaining experience and finding out, in fact, whether they have the ability. With the best will in the world, not many have the necessary attributes and emotional stamina. In any case, it is vital to have some sort of indemnity insurance, particularly if, as is expected, legislation goes ahead that will give clients legal recourse to obtain damages. If a caller, or one of his family, feels that the helpline has played a part in causing physical or emotional damage, at present the plaintiff has to prove his case. It may be that, in future, that the helpline has to prove its innocence, which could be difficult and extremely expensive.

I feel that I have been less than complementary to the Beaumont Society in previous references, but, for all its ways, it is the foremost helping organisation in the country, having been established for twenty five years, and is the only truly national one. Those who have progressed so far that they no longer feel the need for it, might consider continuing their membership, looking on it as their favourite charity.

Membership consists, to a large extent, of "stay-at-homes", with communication provided by a magazine, the Beaumont

Bulletin. In the words of the Society: "It is the Society's own magazine, issued free to members every other month. It contains articles, features and letters contributed by members and their wives, and provides a forum in which members can participate. It provides a life-line to those members who do not feel they can take part in social activities." For those that do not feel that they can receive mail at home, there is the Post Office private box service. There are, in many towns, accommodation address services, and some local groups will allow the use of their address.

In fact, it is ideal for someone just "coming out", who may not wish to attend meetings. It has voluntary officers in most part of the country. Security is paramount and members names and addresses are known only to a few committee members. Communication between members and officers is through the contact system, which is secure, but frustratingly long-winded.

There are three other large groups which produce fairly regular newsletters. These are The TV/TS Group, founded by Yvonne Sinclair and based in London; the Northern Concord, based in Manchester and Transessex, in Essex.

The main disadvantage of any of these groups is that the transvestite has to "come out" first. He has to declare himself, and become a member, for that is their source of income. Should anyone have to "come out" all the way to find the support that he needs? Apart from the question of the advisability of this in all cases, no guidance appears to be given about how to proceed next.

There are a number of organisations approaching the problem independently of each other, most of them short of money. It really is a pity that they can't work together. But this is another example of the transvestite's egoism. First there was the Beaumont Society, then the TV/TS Group split away, followed by the Northern Concord. Some time after that, several members departed, to form the Seahorse Group.

Even within a group there are periodic pogroms. SHAFT, the organisation for transexuals has split into two. There was an abortive attempt to start a federation called GAIN, but the reaction was lukewarm. The idea is still there, faintly. One day all transvestites will get together, to speak with one voice.

I was talking to the wife of one of the TV's, a newcomer to the scene, after a national conference organised by the Beaumont Trust, at which representatives of every group were present. She said "Yes, I enjoyed it and found it worthwhile. But I was amazed at the general air of cattiness. I thought I'd left that behind in female society." It would seem that many TV's take on the worst aspects of the perceived female stereotype, along with the other features. If transvestism is a conflict of self, then it is likely that TV's will be self-centred, and many TS's totally so. Some apparently successful TS's have adopted a lifestyle that is inherently selfish, but the TV's and TS's who have achieved success as people, whether they have changed over or not, seem to be those that have learned to look outside of themselves.

The Beaumont Trust is a registered charity, consisting of various professional counsellors and others, located in various parts of the country, and it has very little public visibility. It has a box address in London, and a telephone helpline open for two evenings a week.

Apart from the Beaumont Trust, none of the societies offers counselling, nor befriending in the strict meaning of the word. The Beaumont Society insists on a meeting with an Area Officer, called "sponsorship" before the "neophyte" can become a full member, but this is mainly to protect the Society and its members.

That the transvestite groups are, increasingly, getting their message across is demonstrated by the fact that they are able to associate themselves with professional and semi-professional groups, like the Council for Voluntary Services and various self-help associations around the country.

There is a tremendous movement in community care to involve voluntary and self-help groups with carers such as Social Services and Community Health services. Some paid workers see this as a threat to their jobs, and some feel that, having spent many years in training, they shouldn't listen to "amateurs". Increasingly the self help groups are being seen a complementary to the statutory services, in that they provide an insight into problems through their life experience. At the same time groups, like the Derby Self Help Team, which is part of Derby CVS, assist the self help groups become professional in their approach, by advising on organisation, accounting and approaching the media. In addition they provide training courses in listening skills, elementary counselling and so on.

The Derby Self Help Team presently encompasses over a hundred groups, from Adult stammerers and Alzheimers Disease, to Women's Growth. Together they can promote the message of the self help movement. People recovering from illness can do so positively, while a positive approach to emotional problems can prevent them becoming ill in the first place. The vast sum of money being spent on promoting physical health, will be wasted unless people feel emotionally willing to obtain the benefit of it.

Chapter 19
PROFESSIONAL SERVICES

What professional help is there for the Transvestite and his partner?

The most obvious source, of course, is the General Practitioner. Sadly, the record of many GP's, certainly in the past, as recorded in the internal newsletters of TV and TS societies is not good. The GP, of course, may have known the patient for many years. For the patient to say that he is Transvestite would come as a considerable shock. But the TV may well be at the limit of his courage and, moreover, under pressure from his family. He will be abnormally sensitive to the GP's reaction. A slight tenseness, a lifting of the eyebrows, by the GP, and all the guilt will flood in.

Some GP's, however, tend to take an opposite line, that is, to minimise it. Transvestism is a manifestation of a sexual, or gender, disturbance, which the patient feels strongly enough about, to approach his doctor.

The GP is also in a difficult position. The aim of his patient is to find some sort of cure. He may ask to be made to stop, but can he be made to want to stop? The GP may, quite reasonably, feel diffident about proposing a solution (to keep on dressing), that is perceived to be socially unacceptable. Often tranquillisers are prescribed. I don't have to dwell on the dangers of their prolonged use and they are, of course, only a short term solution.

The other solution that was often tried, by general psychiatrists was aversion therapy, which is now largely discredited. The theme of this book is that transvestism is often the symptom of something deeper than just dressing up. If this is accepted, then any treatment which only sets out inhibit the cross-dressing, will only approach the symptom and not the cause. If it is, in fact, the mind's own attempt to resolve an emotional conflict, what alternative outlet might it take?

Some GP's, nowadays, are suggesting that their patients take counselling. I shall return to this subject at the end of this chapter, but I wonder whether many TV's or TS's, in fact, continue in counselling for very long.

What can give the GP an even greater shock, is for his patient to announce that he wishes to attend a Gender Identity Clinic. Particularly if the patient concerned is a big, butch man, looking nothing like a woman, the reaction may be for the GP to scoff, which has happened in the author's experience. The point must be made that the people, who work in such clinics, are experienced psychiatrists and do not see their function as solely to change people over.

There is no reason why someone with a gender problem should not have the opportunity to talk things over with someone who stands outside, but understands what he is saying, from having listened to hundreds of other TV's.

I mentioned, earlier, the air of mystery that always surrounded gender reassignment. Gender consultants have always been deeply concerned that, if more was known about the "sex change", then an increasing number of men (and women) who felt unable to cope, for all sorts of reasons, would see reassignment as a way out.

There is a medical concept called Iatrogenesis, which is described as the effect of a physician's words or actions being translated by the patient into the feeling that he has certain symptoms relating to a certain illness. But the definition can be broadened. How many conditions are described now that were unheard of fifty years ago? People possibly suffered them as they came, and may have lived and died without anyone knowing why they felt the way they did. Some illnesses, of course, may have become more widespread due to changing life styles in our Society - heart disease and obesity, for example.

I can remember, when I was young, people suffered from backache, and endured it. Then someone discovered that vertebra in the spine sometimes became misplaced, causing inflammation of the cartilage. Suddenly, everyone you knew had a "slipped disc" and it became a "fashionable illness".

Thus, consultants have always maintained an air of mystery about transexualism, and agreed a policy of keeping the general public in ignorance. One even went as far as to threaten to terminate his client's treatment if he spoke to the press. But, as they say, the cat is out of the bag, and in the worst way. Successive transexuals have interviewed news-papers and magazines and written books. News of the hormones has trickled out. The underground magazines are full of stories and pictures of transexuals and of men being feminised. Certain clinics advertise widely. The media seizes on the "newsy" aspects of the situation. The result is that there is wide dissemination of information, much of it inaccurate, some of it untrue.

The request for reassignment is particularly difficult to gainsay, for there are few concrete symptoms. By now, most prospective transexuals have learnt the right things to say. But they may also have genuinely reclassified events and emotions in their past lives in such a way as reinforce their conviction that reassignment is what they want. On the other hand, there are hundreds of people who are in genuine difficulty and even if they will never be candidates for "the op", they need help.

There seems to be an attitude, in some quarters, of "screen-ing out" transvestites, as though there is some pre-conceived notion of what a transexual is, and those that are rejected seem to be left to sink or swim. To my mind, anyone with a gender problem should receive help. In truth, one's gender identity is unimportant. What one needs is to find a role in life in which one can live with peace of mind. Perhaps they should, instead, be called Gender Role Clinics.

The central theme of this book has been that it is simply a matter of degree and the only question that anyone needs is "Do I really need to change over?"

There a number of commercial ventures, which have done a great deal in desensitising the public to Transvestism. They provide an opportunity for TV's, who are too embarrassed to use normal sources, to shop and take advantage of various facilities, in privacy, at a price.

It is easy for someone to lose his normal 'Shopper's Common Sense'. He has probably travelled some distance, and gone to considerable trouble. Suddenly, he is in an Alladin's Cave, where he can browse and buy without embarrassment. As with any shopping, one should have a clear idea of one's requirements beforehand and resist impulse purchases. It is better to go away empty-handed than to be less than satisfied with one's purchases, or regretting the amount one has spent.

These shops concentrate heavily on the fetishistic and masochistic aspect and, like any sex shops, do not provide any emotional support. By concentrating so heavily on the fetishistic aspect, perhaps, the hope is that there will not be any erosion of the TV's masculine identity, but many transvestites find the blatant approach distinctly off-putting. The recent publicity, particularly in relation to prostitution, is likely to drive the closet TV even deeper into the closet.

The preparations that are claimed to produce physiological changes, such as the prevention of beard growth, are probably worthless. To be strong enough to have any real effect, they would have to be controlled by a doctor's prescription. In any case, one would probably have to continue using them, at around £1000 a year, for as long as one wanted to be a TV. Presumably, those that are applied to the surface are classed as cosmetics, those that are taken internally, as foods. One would think that they contravene the accepted standards of advertising and trading, but actual proof is difficult.

What worries reputable consultants and surgeons, is that a doctor does not have to have any specialist qualifications to practise cosmetic surgery in Great Britain. There are only a few surgeons in this country capable of creating an acceptable vagina, and they are not likely to be found outside hospitals that are part of the NHS. While there is no record of any of the less reputable hospitals carrying out major operations, there have been several horror stories of breast implants going wrong. It is possible that some people go to the "cowboy operators" to avoid having to discuss the matter with their GP, but they should, at least, deal only with services approved by the British Association of Aesthetic Plastic Surgeons. In such a sensitive issue, many consultants and counsellors will give an initial interview without reference to a GP, and will provide a letter for him. Private consultation should not cost a small fortune. From reputable sources, usually associated with a National Health Hospital, it is likely to cost less than £100 a quarter, including medication.

If the medical profession does not regard it as a medical problem, the alternative is to recommend that a patient should see a counsellor, to help him decide why he does it. Cassell, in 1978, wrote that illness is what a patient feels when he goes to the doctor and disease is what he has when he comes away. The emphasis is on the doctor being the expert and labelling the patient with a diagnosis. The patient, too, thinks of a condition, transvestism, and looks for a cure, or transexualism, for which the cure is seen to be the "sex change".

I think that some people shy away from counselling because they feel that their lives are going to be taken over, but the cornerstone of counselling is that everyone has the right to control their own destiny. To most people, counselling implies the giving of advice, as for instance, an investment counsellor, who is usually trying to sell something. Those counsellors working under the auspices of the British Association for Counselling, are, therefore, understandably nervous about the appellation, but find it difficult to decide on another.

In past ages, we lived in small communities, and each member helped another. Now we live relatively lonely lives, keeping a distance from one another, relying on a remote and impersonal welfare state to provide our support. It is a symptom of today that we pay someone to listen to us. But few of us have friends so close that we can share our deepest problems. The problem is, of course, that we will be meeting them again, possibly every day. Although most counsellors are in private practice, their charges are usually very reasonable, often scaled to their client's ability to pay.

The reaction of people to the idea of counselling is that they may appear 'odd', 'a bit funny' or 'not coping'. Negative judgements are made about being "mental". Counselling is not about "mental illness", but about "mental well-being", a positive attitude. There are many people who, sometimes, find life too much for them. Why shouldn't they have the cheek to go out and do something about it?

A counsellor is a best friend who will listen to you, constructively, but one that you can decide never to see again, if you don't want to. Counsellors usually suggest that their client to joins in what is called a contract, an agreed number of meetings for an agreed fee. The contract may be terminated or extended at any time, but it should be by joint discussion.

either the client may feel that he is not getting the help he feels he needs, or the counsellor feels that the limit of the help that can be offered, has been reached.

Rather than concentrating on the cross-dressing as an issue, the emphasis will be on the clients' life skills, on his emotional makeup, on the emotional binds that he has. It is two people working together to focus on the 'healthy', rather than the 'sick', and the emphasis is on the 'good' things that people do for themselves. There is exploration of the past, and some reliving of events, not with the idea of apportioning blame, but as a way of understanding the present. I would suggest that, for many people, their first counselling session is such an unexpected experience, that they wonder what has been achieved. They may feel it worth committing themselves to, say, half a dozen sessions, however, until they discover what the counselling experience means to them.

The author feels somewhat nervous about transexuals who are setting themselves up as counsellors, unless they have had several years general experience, to undertake the necessary in-depth therapy. Certainly, they should demonstrate accreditation by a responsible professional body, such as the BAC or the BPS.

Many TV's and TS's have had a rough ride in childhood. To deal with issues that may go back into infancy, there has to be a very special relationship between the counsellor and client, with an absolute confidence and trust, and an absolute faith that the outcome will be good.

Counsellors, as part of their training and in their practice, themselves, undertake psychotherapy, because they may find that they are bringing their own emotional issues into the counselling relationship. The trouble is that it is such a primitive condition, and so far outside most people's experience, that it is difficult for anyone to take it seriously.

The difficulty is in disabusing people of the idea that the TV can somehow "not do it". Indeed, a male counsellor, if he has not come across a transvestite before, may, without realising it, find it offends his own manhood and he may have to work at dealing with his own emotional reactions.

Writers have been making the point recently that each individual's definitions of gender begin from an early age, and a counsellor may have to confront his, or her, own identity as a man or woman. It is suggested that the difficulties may well be compared to those in cross-cultural work. However there are increasing numbers of TV's and couples approaching counselling organisations such as RELATE.

The tendency is for the client to think in terms of a "condition" that requires a "diagnosis" for which a "cure" will be found. The essence of counselling is to move from a condition-centred approach to a person-centred one. In other words, it is the person himself that matters, not what he is. The aim is for the clients to work out their own solutions, by discussing them with the counsellor.

Counselling may well have an unexpected outcome. The TV may, initially, focus on the idea of stopping dressing, but in the end, decide to enjoy it in innocence, setting out to develop both roles, perhaps finding a new assertiveness and a feeling of being in control of his life. A counsellor may feel disappointed that, at the end of it, the client may still want gender reassignment, but can feel happy if a positive life-plan has been worked out. Many potential transexuals feel irked at the attitude of their consultant, and I believe that if they had spent some time in counselling, the consultant might prove more helpful.

Chapter 20
THE FUTURE

To all those non-TV's, who I hope are reading this book, I'd like to say, "Whatever you may think of my ideas, I hope I have convinced you that transvestism is not a trivial thing. When all is said and done, what we have is a fellow human being in trouble. Can we, then, pass by on the other side?"

When repressed it becomes an obsession, when there is freedom to pursue it, it is a compulsion. Out of the closet it becomes no more than a need. There appears to be no cure, for it is not now seen as an illness. The only therapy that works is acceptance of oneself as one is, but nobody can tell people how to live their lives. All one can do is to offer the example of others and hope that the TV can use it to come to terms with himself.

In the end, whatever theories we put forward, it is an escape. As such, if handled properly, it can be treated as a hobby, somewhat unusual, I admit, and a relaxation. If transvestites can find in themselves the best aspects of both woman and man, that can be no bad thing.

Professionally, transvestism is seen as a paraphilia. The gay community sees it as an offshoot and is resentful of claims that transvestites are not latent homosexuals. The media portrays it as a game played by harmless eccentrics, while feminists see us as an insult. It would seem that everyone has their own view of gender and sexuality, which is refracted through the lens of the person's own identity as a speaker, a writer, an observer or a participant. We are, of course, all participants and we all interpret what's written in our own way.

I don't set out, necessarily, to please people with what I write. On the other hand, I wouldn't willingly hurt anyone's feelings. Some of those, who read books about transvestism, seem to be disappointed that there are no proposals for a cure.

Others seem to feel that there is something wrong about a very 'feminine' male, though they see nothing wrong in a very 'masculine' female - a tomboy. The real question is why such a person is expected to label parts of himself as feminine and why he can only express them as a woman. Much clinical research seems to based on the idea that someone, who cannot conform, is guilty, when the definition of masculinity and femininity is no more than a social construct.

It would be so much easier if there was a clearly defined therapeutic path to 'cure' someone. Perhaps this is why many people seize on the transexual option. Transvestism is an individual experience, as different to each person as his identity and his individual life history.

Because of this individuality, the one over-riding necessity was for this book to be non-directive. The aim is to propose questions, ones that the reader may already be asking himself, and be relieved that he, or she, is not alone in asking them. If the statistics say that there are likely to be 250,000 transvestites in this country. Where are they? There cannot be more than a few thousand that are members of established groups. Very few appear in public. Still fewer appear in the papers, or in the Courts. Many live in fear, secrecy and guilt, as has been described. Increasingly, they are seeking counselling relationships, often accompanied by their partners. Many more dress, quietly at home, with innocent enjoyment. This book is very much the story of my own 'coming out', but I submit that they have asked themselves many of the same questions and found their own answers.

Sometimes the question is asked, "Why shouldn't a man wear a dress?" Women nowadays wear trousers, although there was initially a great deal of opposition. Scots wear the kilt and the Romans wore skirts, of a kind, conquering most of the known world. In view of the foregoing, this seems a trivial argument, until you remember that clothing is a personal statement. When a woman wears trousers, she says "I am being practical". She isn't saying "I am a man". Even a woman's two piece suit normally has a feminine cut, or little touches of femininity about it. But, if a woman decides to go out in mannish jeans, a sweatshirt and a short, spiky haircut with no makeup, people might look, but they wouldn't be unduly worried.

Until the 60's, there were rules about women's dress, though not as limiting as those for the men. They were imposed by the fashion houses and were commercially exploitative. Since then, women have challenged practically every rule. I submit that this is a symptom of their emerging awareness of themselves, and their increasing insistence on expressing themselves, as individual self-motivated people. At one time they were told not to wear high heels with trousers, and that only certain women should wear trousers. Both of these rules have been successfully challenged. The restricted dress of men means that they are less subject to age-ist conventions, but women of all ages are now wearing ski pants, even leggings, and looking good in them. I have recently seen men wearing leggings but they wear gaudy sweatshirts with them, to make it clear that they have a bicycle nearby.

Experimentation for males is restricted to the young and, even then, it has taken the form of uniforms: Teddy boys, Mods, Rockers, Hippies, Punks and so on. It seems that social grouping is more important to males, an extension of the gang ethos of boyhood. For many people, a uniform is camouflage to hide behind in social conformity.

Other social signals have been green wellies for people who have 'a place in the country', or shell suits for middle class families on holiday. At work, uniforms identify people, to assist customers, or they may express a corporate image. Some companies take this to such an extent that one wonders if there is a dependence on image to compensate for lack of substance in the product.

A TV friend of mine said, recently "I've been meaning to buy some new trousers for work. But I know in advance how they'll fit and what they'll look like. I just haven't been able to work up any enthusiasm." A man can now have keepers in his ears, but woe betide him if he wears nice dangly ones!

Yet personal adornment and personal expression is every person's right. If Society labels such innocent enjoyment feminine, it is hardly surprising that the transvestite labels himself feminine. On the other hand, many transvestites could not allow themselves to wear even keepers in their male guise.

Gender motivation is a part of everyone's life, whether it causes problems or not. If there are people, who are totally masculine in their outlook, that are forever trying to conform to an unrealistic macho role model, perhaps they are subject to frustrations of their own. Looking at the exaggerated stereotypes portrayed by the media, that are becoming role models for too many people, perhaps Society has a gender problem.

Psychology makes a clear distinction between the development of self and the development of interpersonal relationships. They develop concurrently, but separately. I see gender, therefore, as part of the view one has of oneself as a person, while sexuality arises out of the way one interacts with people of the same or opposite kind.

"He is a man, therefore I must compete with him. She is a woman, therefore I must protect her, or patronise her" (depending on your point of view). Because of my feeling, that the kind of transvestism described in this book is primarily a matter of self expression, the term heterosexual transvestite becomes a nonsense, and I prefer to use Bancroft's title, the Dual Role Transvestite.

The idea that sexuality is who we go to bed with, produces a fundamental confusion. Psychologists mean something quite different. They are talking about the whole system of behaviours and attitudes that begin with our heredity and are related to our biological sex. Thus it becomes an umbrella term involving perceptions that people have about themselves and others (gender), and the way people deal with each other and their relationships, as well as their sexual orientation.

I have tried to avoid talking about 'identity' for the same reason. Many people suggest that it is something we might be born with and carry, fixed and invariable throughout our lives.

Bem defines gender identity as "The degree to which one regards oneself as male or female", not just the idea that one is a man or a woman. In order to do so, as children, we each must have compared ourselves to others, who demonstrated their definition of 'manly' and 'womanly'. They in turn, derived this from others - from the culture of which they were a part, and their own individual experiences.

This is the stereotype, which comes from outside, either imposed or offered. The more authoritarian the source, the more it becomes what one ought to feel rather than what one really feels. From the conflict between gender identity, often called the core identity, and gender stereotype is produced what Bem calls the gender schema, as a part of one's whole cognitive reaction to life and experience. The more things that are defined as masculine and feminine, the more they will be forced into the gender subset of one's total schema.

My feeling is that the word schema, itself, is so much more expressive of everyday reality than the word identity. It emphasises that there is no such thing as perfectly male and perfectly female, but a continuum, based on a diversity of people's heredity, a diversity of growing experiences and a diversity of social attitudes. Moreover, it emphasises something that is flexible, that can change and be built on in response to changing feelings, especially with age.

It would, perhaps, be illuminating to find, say, that transvestism and transexualism is more prevalent in one

country than in another, or that it affected one area of Society more than another, industry versus the arts, for instance. It may be that it is seen as a problem by the 'victims' and the general public, not to mention the 'professionals' simply as a consequence of our Western society. Perhaps it simply has no sociological relevance in other cultures. So many men find that they cannot express emotions, yet it is emotional responses that provide the drive to invent, to create and to innovate. To succeed in anything requires enthusiasm and inspiration. A man achieves most when he loves his work. The many creators in this world, architects, designers, artists, musicians, are expressing emotions that could be said to be feminine, although there are no figures to say that there are less TV's among them, than among those pursuing less obviously artistic careers. I once thought to myself, "If I had any talent as a musician, I wouldn't be a TV", and shortly after, met three TV's who were, or who had been, professional musicians. Perhaps, although they used some part of their qualities, the making of music didn't exercise the full range of emotion that their personalities needed to express.

The very fact that different TV's give different accounts, and that for other people similar accounts are not associated with transvestism, should tell us that there is not one single cause. The common factor in many transvestite's lives does however appear to be that it is not just the 'femininity' of the boy or man, but the narrowness of the stereotype offered to him and the pressure to conform to it.

For practically every emotional disturbance that we suffer as grown-ups, our parents seem to be blamed. But parents have enough trouble surviving in their own lives; mostly they do their best within their own emotional structure. Except in rigid and authoritarian families, children influence the parents at least as much as the parents influence the children. In any case, children are immensely adaptable and will adapt if allowed to do so. It is usually suggested that, if the child can merge with its peer group, everything will be alright.

But is this necessarily true? Schools, in general, have become more crowded and anonymous. Teachers struggle to give individual attention, against economic pressures to teach by rote. Until recently, little was done about the playground, yet it is here that children learn more than they ever do in the classroom. Those who can't, or won't, conform to playground society can't escape. Children are exposed to school for most of their most impressionable ten years, and learn about life and relationships, with their own and the other sex.

But the school and the peer group can only be a reflection of the attitudes of the community which it serves. Studies have shown that lower SES children hold more stereotyped views about gender roles, but one could equally suggest that it is a feature of most schools, particularly public schools.

Too often, shy and sensitive boys are labelled as 'sissy' by their peer group, often their parents and teachers, and even some psychiatrists. They may be rejected completely and grow up as transexuals and solitaries, unable to negotiate successful relationships, either personal or sexual.

Or they manage to conform, later becoming transvestites, unable to express their whole selves in only their biological gender role. Such rigid and inflexible ideas about gender appear in all sorts of guises. They may prevent the boy from being who he is, instead forcing him into narrow tram tracks of behaviour and feeling, but they affect you, me, everyone, to a greater or lesser degree.

It may be internalised in the child just as surely as the feeling that his sexual preference is somehow 'natural', rather than learned. We are learning that exclusive heterosexuality is not as universal as we thought; it may be that TV's are more rigidly heterosexual than most people. It could be that such attitudes are a factor in exclusive homosexuality; the idea that somebody must be one thing or the other.

Such attitudes may be responsible for research into physiological and genetic factors, which make men and women different, where these are said 'feminise' boys and 'masculinise' girls, especially where this is seen as a search for a 'cure' for transexualism (and also for being gay), or to legitimise it. Let us suggest that all that this shows is that there is a natural variation in both boys and girls; and nobody has yet demonstrated how a boy can become homosexual, transexual, or simply a gentle man. Indeed, what science, as typified by the work of Edelman, is also proving is what we always knew, that each one of us is a unique individual.

Certainly, if we are thinking of genetic or foetal endocrine intervention, isn't there a danger that we could breed out our 'gentle' men, our poets and philosophers, even counsellors and psychodynamicists? It is one thing to intervene in physical ailments, but quite another to do so in response to social values that may themselves be suspect.

Much women's clothing is designed to be sexually attractive to men, of course, and is attractive to some men because it is women's clothing. But, in trying on something lacy and flimsy, they may experience the physical and emotional sensation of wearing something pretty for the first time. They may feel the silkiness of tights, or the feeling of earrings dangling. What, for women, is an everyday experience, is entirely new to the man.

Every human being has a natural urge to dress up, to enjoy experimenting with personal adornment, strange fabrics and the exploration of all the senses. This is the right of every person, yet it is denied to many male children and adults.

The ability to do so, and to experience physical sensations, is, for them, labelled feminine. In cross dressing, a TV may allow himself a whole range of feelings that are too subtle to name, but ones that his individual environment has taught him are not permissible for a man.

My personal view is that very few transvestites, even if they find it an erotic experience, dress for this reason initially. The transition to sexual arousal may be as fast as thought, or take years, as with childhood experimentation. Many adult men said that they found themselves trying on some clothes, often after a crisis, like divorce or bereavement. They dress for one reason or another first, and may *then* find it sexually exciting. The important question is why they dress and only the individual person can answer that, assuming the experience is not too painful to recall. Usually, it is a solitary ritual, labelled as narcissistic. But isn't narcissism a natural human motivation? It is an intrinsic part of presenting one's self to the world. If you feel good about yourself, people react in a positive way.

Fetishism seems to be no problem for women, because nobody thinks anything of it. No-one could reasonably suggest that a twenty inch mini-skirt is practical or even comfortable. A woman will say she wears it because she feels nice. Where is the boundary between feeling nice and feeling sexy?

It must be admitted that a reason women have not translated fetishism into sexual fantasy might be because they have always been told that they must not be sexual people, but romantic. In contrast, men are told they must be highly sexual people, but then are given no outlet for it.

Yet women are increasingly insisting on their right to sexuality. The last few weeks have seen the publication of a porn magazine for women and there is the success of the Chippendales. What about the female partner in a female domination fantasy?

Although this book has dealt with male transvestites, there are female to male transvestites and transexuals. The reason why they are not so common is unclear, nor why there is an increasing number of women contemplating gender reassignment. In recent years, women's role in Society has been brought into question. Yet, perhaps it is men's role that needs to change.

In Society today, the average man's function seems to be no more than someone who does a job of work and produces wealth for his company. To many people, the sole criterion when judging him, is the material well-being he has generated for his family. The size of his house, whether he can afford a leather three piece suite, or can provide an en suite bathroom. Because very few jobs, or lifestyles, give pride in achievement, the emphasis turns to pride in material things, or aggressiveness at inappropriate moments, such as when driving a car.

A woman may be an assertive, competitive, business person in her daily life, yet can go home and relax from this mode. Men seem to have to continue this assertiveness and competitiveness in their relaxation hours. They compete in their interactions, they have to top each other in conversation. In the pub, they set out to tell the tallest stories. You might think it nice to spend a quiet day, fishing by the river, yet many men have to measure themselves against their peers in angling competitions. My family once had a boat, with the idea of spending time pottering about. I soon realised that the only way I could get it onto the water, would be to join a club and enter races, leaving my family kicking their heels on the bank. Men have to be assured, self-sufficient, independent - and lonely.

I once countered a suggestion that TV's were immature by giving the example of a successful businessman, boss of a thousand people by his own efforts, admired by all, yet, if you mentioned the words 'employee relations' to him, he would look at you blankly. Who is immature? TV's, in general, are not 'failed men'. The diversion of attention in the closet can often mean a TV does not reach his full potential, but many are high ranking officers and civil servants, company directors and leaders in their field. I know TV's that have served, with distinction, in the armed services, the Fire Brigade and the Police.

There are tremendous changes in women's roles going on in Society at the moment. Traditionally, a wife depended very heavily on her husband. To face life alone was a daunting prospect, especially if there were children to look after. Nowadays, women are more able to support themselves and earn a living, one parent families are becoming more and more common. The corollary of this is that the husband may feel that he isn't needed any more. Indeed, there have been militant feminists saying this very thing. But, when we think of a couple, with the wife going out to work, we still think in terms of role reversal. We talk about a 'house husband' and the stereotype is effectively the same.

In order to succeed, men must be strong, courageous, competitive, ambitious and assertive (not aggressive). Because, in our culture, it is the man who has to provide, these attributes are necessary to him, and are the prized positive features of masculinity. This, I wouldn't argue with. But he is given no chance to drop out of this mode. There are many positive features in femininity as well.

While, on the surface, women criticise the male ethos, underneath they encourage it. Many still look for someone to be strong, the lord and master to protect them and provide for a family. Society is giving men conflicting signals of what is required of them. Many react by becoming more stereotyped or more macho. An unbalance has been created and the role that men find themselves in is so rigid that they find they cannot change.

Women's groups complain about lack of freedom, yet men are not free either. It may be true that women are limited in their range of actions, yet they are relatively free to express themselves. Men have freedom of action, yet have a limited freedom of expression. Could it be that, with transvestites this, unknowingly, finds its outlet in role play?

Meanwhile, in the closet, feelings that cannot be expressed take on a whole new urgency. They may be safely tucked away in denial and suppression for years, then surface in times of stress. If the TV cannot have these feelings as a man, he may unthinkingly begin to express them as a woman. When he does, the pressures that told him he mustn't have those feelings as a man also tells him he mustn't act them out as a woman. A system may be set up, where feelings of 'not being a man' conflict with urge to dress, followed by a session of relief dressing, followed by a reaction in becoming over-macho, followed in turn by guilt, in a downward spiral of emotional distress. The need becomes an obsession, distracting from everyday life. Efforts to control, like 'wardrobe burning', fail repeatedly. The person may attempt other escapes, through alcohol, drugs, tranquillisers, workaholism. He will tell lies and will become less 'present' for his family. Even in the face of direct confrontation he will deny the problem, even the physical fact of the cross dressing. The feelings that are the source of the cross dressing urge are also the source of the guilt - a classical Catch 22 situation.

This, of course, has all the hallmarks of addiction, and it is often labelled as such. One obvious difference is that chemical addiction usually produces physiological changes, often such as to perpetuate the addiction. It is arguable that, in this 'closet' situation, cross dressing produces similar psychological changes, leading to a loss of value for the male life and a glamorisation of the female life. But the vital difference is that addiction is often an escape from feelings, while cross dressing may, in part, be an enactment of them.

The feelings which are evoked contrast with a male life that may well be very humdrum and boring. For many men, it is, in any case, a strange experience to 'feel' and some can allow themselves to experience the strong feelings that women arouse in them. It is usual to dress as someone, and so there could be an element of identification with an admired, or loved person. Sometimes the TV will attach to a particular person's clothes, or those from a certain period, sometimes the symbol of that person, sometimes taking her as a role model.

He is not identifying himself as female, or as that person, but recognising common attributes that in the man are denied expression. This can produce a great deal of confusion, especially if a growing number of 'female' attributes are attached and a growing number of 'male' ones are rejected. It is hardly surprising if they grow into an alternative female self, initially a fantasy, then becoming more and more real. From being an alternative schema it becomes the more desirable one. The TV may feel "If I were a woman, I could have these feelings all the time and no one would mind", forgetting that women don't have such feelings all the time and that their lives can be very humdrum and boring. There is a world of difference between believing one is a woman and not being happy as a man.

It worries me that, though we give permission, it isn't sufficient, and it can cause as much trouble as it saves. The TV newly 'out' has to find his own way, often a long and lonely process. Permission to have feelings implies the need to learn how to have them. To 'come out' too quickly may be as dangerous as not coming out at all. Many TV's have a macho reaction after their session as a 'female'. The further they go into the role, particularly if pushed, or led on, initially, the more extreme the reaction is likely to be. On two occasions I have observed this to be extremely violent. Somehow, they have to experience this other life that they have permission for, while keeping one foot in reality and not getting swept away in the fantasy. Either getting into situations they aren't prepared for, or being dazzled by the enthusiasm of pre-op TS's busy planning for their 'sex change'.

Some TV's and their wives seem to go beyond the concept of role play and dressing-up games. They both seem to find inner strength from a positive and flexible view of life.

They accept each other's whole selves so completely that their marriage becomes a true sharing. It becomes a literal fact that the husband does not always have to 'wear the trousers'; from time to time, neither of them have to.

Could the TV, by psychotherapy, counselling or otherwise, merge these two schemas into one?

Just as we don't really know how many TV's there are, we don't know how many have stopped. After all, they aren't going to burn their bridges by saying so publicly.

People's gender schemata go back to the first few months of their lives. To change the very bases of them may mean re-evaluating their whole cognitive structure. Can people change their whole lives in such a drastic way?

Such a result of therapy may, be unexpected and wholly unwelcome. The TV may have built his whole life around a very macho persona. Can someone in a very masculine and aggressive career become gentle and nurturing? If he sets out to change what are, after all, the foundations of his life, does he run the very real risk of jeopardising his whole lifestyle by modifying something so fundamental? The TV's wife may see him as a very masculine man and not want someone more gentle in his approach to life. Had the childhood of Monica Jay's hero, in *Geraldine* been different, he probably wouldn't have become a successful executive. He might, however, have become a very good counsellor.

Better, perhaps, to build both roles independently, and if he gets the best of both worlds, why not? But, after the initial round of clubbing and pubbing, most TV's retire quietly to dress, from time to time, in their homes, as and when they feel like it.

What the TV gains is the power to choose when and where and how he will dress. The freedom to be himself, with the responsibility to avoid distress to others.

In the end, it doesn't matter what clothes one likes to wear or what role one adopts, so long as one is able to gain a positive and forward moving lifestyle.

If we had a society that could accept people for themselves as valuable individuals, whether they were children or adults, instead of forcing them to be what we think they 'ought' to be, transvestism *as we know it* might disappear, people might be clearer about their sexuality, and transexuals might have a clearer idea of themselves much earlier in life and be able to do something about it.

The man of the future could be at once emotional, considerate and nurturing, strong yet empathetic, valuing humanity over money and power; a gentle man yet a fearsome Rugby player. He will play hard and work hard, but will always have a clear idea of himself and his direction in life. To paraphrase Sandra Bem's view of the ideal future, "That men and women will always be different from each other, but that each individual will be able to find the best within their self, regardless of whether we now define it as masculine or feminine."

But any solution, derived from modifying social attitudes, must be a long term one. In the short term, it must not be assumed that the streets will be filled with men in dresses and funny wigs. Transgendered people are said to comprise about one percent of the population. Those that have come out in public view have mostly done so quietly, when they were allowed to do so. By having the image of peaceful human beings who only want to be allowed to live their lives as they wish, while everyone else does the same, perhaps they are stealing a march on the radical feminists and gay people, whose notoriety is hindering them as much as helping. Many of the minority groups are acquiring a guarded acceptance, but then setting themselves apart.

Transvestism and transexualism is becoming more openly discussed. People are taking an interest in gender issues, and in those who experiment in different ways. Is it on the increase, or is it because people feel more able to be open about themselves? Perhaps our Society is becoming less antagonistic towards personal expression, less judgmental. This year has seen someone close to the Royal Family attending parties, while wearing lipstick, with no one really worrying, and an international footballer who broke down and cried on the pitch, to be hailed as a man of the nineties.

The vast majority of TV's dress quietly at home and will probably continue to do so. Others attend the various meetings where there are changing facilities. Some travel 'dressed' to and from the meetings; one can imagine that they drive carefully and make sure their vehicles are in good condition. Interestingly, many report that they automatically drive less aggressively anyway, and many experience what must be women's experiences with male drivers.

For all my rationalisation, there still seems to be a part of me that, as someone said, 'marches to the beat of a different drum'. I no longer think in terms of male and female in relation to myself. Other people can do that. I have given myself permission to have what feelings I like and delight in them, regardless of what clothes I am wearing. I was born a transvestite and I'll die a transvestite, but I don't have to dress up unless I feel like a change. On the other hand, I wish to keep my options open, and insist on one freedom that is supposed to be the prerogative of women - that of changing my mind!

I have played the part of a man. I earned a steady living and helped bring up the children. Perhaps I could have been a better father, but I treasure a letter I had from my eldest son, some time after the divorce. He was away at University when the crisis in our marriage blew up, thus he heard of the details at second hand. For many months I heard nothing from him, so I wrote him a letter. For many more months, I still heard nothing, then a letter arrived from him. He had been appalled and disgusted when he heard the news, but had spent some time thinking it over. He said that he still had difficulty with the idea, but finished the letter by saying "I am proud to have had you and Mum for my parents."

INFORMATION AND CARE PROVIDING ORGANISATIONS.

THE BEAUMONT TRUST

The Beaumont Trust hopes to foster research into both the psychological and social aspects of transvestism and transexualism. The Trust provides speakers for helping organisations eg. Samaritans, Marriage Guidance Counsellors, G.P.s, Personnel Officers, Health Centres, DHSS etc. It also produces literature, can arrange workshops, counsellors, befriending facilities, conferences and information sheets.

The Beaumont Trust includes professionals and members of other relevant organisations as trustees and officers, and attempts to help find appropriate assistance for the gender dysphoric person and his or her relatives and partners. To this end we operate a telephone helpline every Tuesday and Thursday evening from 7pm until 11pm. The telephone number is 0171 730 7453. Alternatively, write to: BEAUMONT TRUST, BM CHARITY, LONDON WC1N 3XX.

THE BEAUMONT SOCIETY

The Beaumont Society is a self help association established in 1965, to facilitate contact between primarily transvestites and gender motivated transexuals. The membership is largely heterosexual, but it is a non sexual organisation - it is about gender and support, not a contact organisation for sexual purposes. It is a social group, and it maintains the individual's security whilst enabling contact to be made. Newsletters are produced by and for the membership. Write to: The Beaumont Society, BM Box 3084, London. WC1N 3XX

WOMEN OF THE BEAUMONT SOCIETY

Women of the Beaumont Society. A wives and partners and family support group, designed to help support those who find their loved one's behaviour difficult to understand. Those seeking further information may write to: Women of the Beaumont Society, BM WOBS, London WC1N 3XX.

THE SEAHORSE SOCIETY.

Those who feel themselves to be Heterosexual Transvestites or Transexuals may wish to write to: BM Seahorse, London WC1N 3XX.

GENDYS NETWORK

GENDYS is a network for all who have encountered gender identity problems personally, transsexuals, transgendered people and gender dysphoric people of either sex, and for those who provide care, both professional and lay.

The network produces a quarterly journal, and holds biennial conferences, the next one being in Autumn 2000.

The aim is to provide confidential help and information, including a contact system, including sources of professional counselling. It also aims to provide support for those who are emotionally close, families, lovers and friends.

The network is to develop a forum for debate and a dialogue between the client group and carers, so that understanding and standards can be improved. It will endeavour to provide information, provoke discussion, thought and understanding, and to help give a fair impression of some of the difficulties often encountered and how they may be dealt with. Gendys Network, BM GENDYS, London WC1N 3XX *http://www.gendys.mcmail.com/*

BRITISH ASSOCIATION FOR COUNSELLING

The Association aims to promote understanding and awareness of counselling throughout Society, increase the availability of counselling by trained and supervised counsellors, maintain and raise standards of counselling training and practice, provide support for counsellors, particularly opportunities for their personal growth, education and training, respond to the increasing demand for information and advice concerning both counselling and counsellors, and represent counselling at national level. British Association for Counselling,

1, Regent Place, Rugby, Warwickshire CV21 2PJ.

THE FORUM CLINIC

A specialist service offering confidential counselling for sexual, gender, marital and relationship problems.
The London Institute for the Study of Human Sexuality,
10, Warwick Road, Earls Court, London SW5 9UH.
Telephone 071 373 0901 (Weekdays 9.30am-5.00pm)

RELATE

Formerly known as the Marriage Guidance Council, RELATE now helps with relationship problems outside and inside marriage, such as loneliness, jealousy, difficulties with parents, in-laws and children. Relationship counselling aims to help single people, couples and families to develop as individuals, as well as to find and develop relationships, helping with personal, emotional and sexual problems. The number of the nearest centre will be found in the local telephone directory.

RELATE, Herbert Gray College, Little Church Street, Rugby, CV21 3AP.

READING LIST

Transvestism, H. Brierley, Pergamon Press (1979)
(This, unfortunately is no longer in print, but can be ordered through your local library)

A Guide to Transsexualism, Transgenderism and Gender Dysphoria, Gendys etwork, BM GENDYS, London WC1N 3XX

Transvestism: A Guide. ed M.T.Haslam.

The Beaumont Trust, BM CHARITY, London WC1N 3XX.

Fantastic Women, Annie Woodhouse, Macmillan

My Husband Wears my Clothes, Peggy J. Rudd Ed.d., PM Publishers, Katy, Texas. (USA)

Cross Dressing with Dignity, Peggy J. Rudd Ed.d, PM Publishers, Katy, Texas. (USA)

Both the above from Lifeworks UK, PO Box 6566, Sutton Coldfield B76 9QZ

Transgender Warriors, Leslie Feinberg, Beacon Press

Transformations, Marriette Pathy Allen, Outreach Book Service, 126, Western Avenue, Suite 222, Augusta ME 04330 (USA)

Geraldine - For the love of a Transvestite, Monica Jay, Mandarin Books.

Men in Petticoats, Peter Farrer, Kam Publications Garstang

In Female Disguise, Peter Farrer, Kam Publications Garstang

Cross dressing, Sex and Gender, Vern and Bonnie Bullough, University of Pennsylvania Press

Transvestites and Transexuals - Towards a theory of cross-gender behaviour, Dr. Richard F. Docter, Plenum Press (USA)

Transvestites - The Erotic Drive to Cross Dress, Magnus Hirschfield M.D. (Translated by Michael A. Lombardi Nash Ph.D.), Prometheus Books (USA) (First publ. 1910)

Vested Interests, Marjorie Garber, Penguin Books